I0158928

It's Still All or Nothing

Jannette S. Williams-Holt

DEDICATION

This book is dedicated to Sylvia Williams, my mother, and best friend. The most beautiful, peaceful, loving, supportive, caring person I know. I also dedicate this book to my precious, loving, angel, Kristina Alicia Livingston. Whose life has taught me that it is not the number of our days lived, but rather the life lived that matters, for in three short years (Kristina) your life has proven to be immeasurable.

In loving, you taught me to love. In giving, you taught me to give. In living joyfully, even in pain and constant hospitalization, you taught me to appreciate life, for you always found something to laugh and smile about. Finally, in dying you both taught me that when you truly love, it's never goodbye, no, just until we meet again.

Looking forward to meeting you both in heaven, keep an eye out for me. Through loving the both of you and Jesus with all my heart, mind, and soul, I now know that heaven will surely be worth all.

CONTENTS

It's Still All or Nothing

IT'S STILL ALL
OR NOTHING

For a long time, I was a Christian of the pew, playing church on Sundays and living like hell throughout the rest of the week. I was shacking up and having kids out of wedlock. My kids' father wanted to get married but that word; marriage gave me a headache, that word literally made me sick to my stomach. I told him there's a lot of women out there looking for a husband, it's okay if you move on to one of them and I meant it. I was just out of a horrible marriage and had no desire of jumping out of the fire, right back into the frying pan. I did not want to hear that word, marriage, and I was okay in my spirit with him moving on.

I was quick-tempered. In addition, I had a good handle on some seventy-five to one hundred and fifty-pound words and I knew just how to sling them. Cursing was such a part of my vocabulary whereas, when I spoke, I was not even aware of it; the words just came out naturally. I was easily agitated, could not stand stupid people, running on with stupid conversations. And in relationships, I was not too forgiving, did not care to hear explanations or justifications, in my mind I thought you know what, I am not your Huckleberry, and I treated situations as such.

Yet, I was in church on Sundays and felt like I was going to heaven. I had no relationship with God, my life was all about me, and my gains.

In the Bible, God said if we fulfill these two commandments then we would have fulfilled them all. First, love the Lord thy God with all thine heart, mind, and soul and second, love thy neighbor as thyself. I did not practice this, said I was a Christian but did not resemble him at all, I probably ran more people away from the church, rather than to the church. Therefore, God allowed Satan to yoke me up, so that he could put me in check.

God had been pricking me in my spirit about my hypocritical Christian relationship with him. Had been telling me that it is all or nothing, but I kept saying not now. I was living like Satan for so long and getting away with it, so why change? There was no apparent consequence of my disobedience. God is long-suffering and full of mercy and grace, but God would not allow any man to make a mockery of him.

God said enough is enough, and he allowed Satan to sift me. This is when I recognized that we are fighting against spiritual forces in high places, for I thought I was tough, but Satan strung me up and wrung me out to dry.

Suddenly attacks were coming from everywhere. It seems like overnight all hell broke loose. My oldest daughter was diagnosed with cancer, while I was in the hospital with her being prep for surgery, I received a telephone call saying my four-month-old had stop breathing, that her lips and nail beds were purple and that she was also in route to the emergency room.

At Miami Children's Hospital, I remember running from the oncology unit to the emergency room like a yo-yo between the two of my kids. One daughter who was newly diagnosed with end-stage neuroblastoma and the other I had not yet a clue as to what was wrong. Two days later, on my way home from the hospital, while riding down I-95, my front tire blew out and my car spun around on the expressway, completely out of control, when the car came to a standstill, I was surprised to find I was still in one piece.

That same day I received notice from my employer that they could no longer accommodate me. I remember walking down the expressway towards the nearest exit, which seemed to be never-ending, cars speeding past me. Thank God for my dark sheds because now tears had been pouring like a fountain. I remember thinking okay, what's next?

Ooh, and there was allot next. Glad we don't see it all coming at us at once because if I did, I might have just sprawl out on the highway and beg the passing motorist to please run over me. I was a new employee at the above-mentioned job but still, I thought the state had laws in place to protect citizens in my situation. People who needed time off for emergent family medical situations, but I soon found out since I was still on probation I could be fired at any time without consequence.

I didn't understand how an employer, seeing my emergent situation would selfishly add to that, but I guess, just like I had been all about me and mines, she was all about her life and her gains as well.

My kids' father lost his job a few weeks earlier, so now I couldn't afford to buy pampers, milk, gas, food or look for employment. For if my daughter was released from the hospital today, it seemed we'll be back in the hospital tomorrow; for excessive nausea and vomiting, a fever, low blood count, and infection or something.

To make matters worse my kids' father and I were no longer friends. We could no longer see eye to eye. We were both under so much pressure that instead of joining hands and forming a circle around our kids, our family and trying to hold each other and the family up; we were pointing fingers and constantly pulling each other down. I felt like we were at that place where we really could no longer stand the sight of each other. We both still loved our kids, looking back now I remember seeing him often with his head bowed down in his hand, complaining of a headache, with reddened eyes, I would know he had been crying and I felt his pain, but we were now untouchable towards each other.

Often, I felt like I should have been doing something, but my hands were so tied, we had to stand back and let the doctors do their do and just pray, which didn't seem to be enough. Now as I look back in retrospect I think he must have felt just as hand tied as I did. We were supposed to protect our kids; how could we just look on and watch them suffer and die? If it were my call, I would have taken her pain. I would have taken her sentence and I would have willed her to live a long and healthy life.

I was running around doing, doing and doing, because I needed to be doing something and I felt like he should have been doing more. However, to me it seemed as if he had already raised his right hand up, with a white handkerchief waving high, screaming, I surrender. Now I noticed that while I was doing even things that probably didn't make too much of a difference, he was always crying, and he hadn't given up but just like me, he just didn't know what to do. Moreover, there was nothing to do, the power of life and death is in the hand of the beholder.

Because of our domino effect, we had to move in with my sister, sleeping on her living room floor. In addition, everything on the car started breaking down. So, every penny we received was going right back out, like a bad curse that we could not crawl out from under.

A few months after my daughter was diagnosed with cancer and was fighting for her life, I came home from the hospital to find my mom who was now my backbone, weak and lethargic, eyes puffy, face black and swollen. Just looking, I knew she too was gravely ill. I took her to the nearest clinic that in turn, took some vital signs, gave her some blood pressure medication, and called an ambulance to have her transferred to Jackson Memorial Hospital.

For the next week, she was coming in and out of consciousness, diagnosed with end-stage renal disease and Hypertensive crisis. She had to have emergency surgery for dialysis assess and consecutively over the next three to four days she had to receive dialysis, in order to rid the toxins from her body that her non-functioning kidneys were no longer able to filter out. We were told that dialysis for her was only a temporary measure and that her long-term survival depended upon her receiving a kidney transplant.

Doctors also said, had she not come in when she did, she would have surely died. So here I was, my daughter in the hospital receiving chemotherapy and needing a double bone marrow transplant and my mother in the hospital needing a kidney transplant; homeless, unemployed, and broke, with absolutely no shoulder to cry on.

To make matters worse every time I got into my car which usually drove smooth, as soon as I approached a four-way stoplight, instead of my brakes holding they would accelerate. I took my car to four different mechanics who could find absolutely nothing wrong. As far as they could see my brakes were working perfectly, this spooked me out because at stop signs or a non-threatening light my car slowed or stopped perfectly. However, at big intersections, they seemed to have a mind of their own. I remember the last time this happened, I had my three kids in the car and I had to swerve off the road to avoid a head-on collision, as a result, I almost split a tree. I remember my car stopping just short of that tree. I could stand in front of my car and touch the car and the tree.

That day, I gathered my kids and walked away from that spooky, damned car. Left it right there by that tree where it came to a halt. Although the mechanics could find nothing wrong with it, I knew there was something crazy going on, there had to be something wrong. Later, someone offered me three hundred dollars for it, it might have been worth more, but I didn't mind, I would have given that coffin up for free.

As I walked down the streets with my three little kids, my heart pounding like it would easily explode, I didn't even care to see a picture of that car again, just felt like I had taken too much of a chance already, felt lucky to have all of my kids with me in one piece. For the first time in my life, didn't mind taking the bus and was happy to be walking. My hands were trembling too much to call anyone, and at that moment, I would have walked from there to Timbuktu. I just needed to feel the breeze against my skin. I needed to gather my thoughts, just needed to breathe, slowly innn and ouuut.

Again, when walking to check the mail one day, while holding my daughter who was just released from the hospital, I heard screaming and turned just in time to find a deranged woman running up behind me with an ice pick. I turned around in time enough to prevent her from killing me, but I still ended up getting defensive jabs from her. I didn't even know this woman, but the police said she was no stranger to them, they had arrested her before. She had psychological issues. She would be baker acted into a mental facility for a few days but then she would be released back onto the streets.

That was scary, crazy people roaming around and it's not their fault, they need supervision. All kind of strange things had been happening. I was riding down one hundred and fifty-six street and northeast six avenues and a car came speeding out of nowhere running me off the streets. If I had not cleared his path in a split second, me, my mom, and my kids would have been killed instantly.

Later, when I went to the doctor for a checkup I was told that my pap smear came back abnormal, requiring further testing to rule out cervical cancer. I was also told upon physical examination that a lump was felt in my right breast and in my abdomen. I was told that I needed to have a breast biopsy and a colonoscopy and was given a card with the number of a specialist for further follow-up.

I remember walking out of that doctor's office thinking, God I ain't no Job, my hands are too short to box with you. If this is what it comes down to, if my life is what you want, then so be it? I am drained, empty, barren, and dry. I have absolutely nothing else to lose. At this point, my daughter had just succumbed to cancer and was buried two weeks prior. Both of my grandfather's maternal and paternal had passed the week after her funeral, within hours of each other and my mother was still in and out of the hospital.

Therefore, at this point, I actually felt like death would be more than welcoming, because the last eighteen months had been a living hell, with one thing after the other. I was tired of fighting, tired of being. Here in I also learned never to judge a book by its cover, for I probably looked as if I was strung out on drugs, but I was just strung out on life. At that moment, I realized that sometimes life is not what we make of it, circumstances beyond our control can sometimes back us up against a wall and that devil will try to place his elbow up under our chin and just hold us there.

This is when I realized that Satan himself was fighting me. That Satan was not only after my sanity but also after my very life. Years later, this was also prophesied to me, that God has great plans for my life and that Satan had been throwing everything he has at me, in order to stop my destiny.

However, I was told by the prophet of God, that God wanted me to know that he has me covered and my purpose will prevail. Looking back now in retrospect I realize, that life is not really what you make of it because you can lose all that you thought you had in the blink of an eye. I realized that life is uncertain and who can truly say, that they're going to go back to sleep just the way they woke up to morning; with nothing significantly changed. The power of life and death is not in our hands. The changes in the weather are not in our hands and now more than ever I have noticed that our very own finances, is not securely in our hands. All are temporal loans. Like Solomon, I have come to notice that fleeting man that we are, we must have reverence for God. Enjoy what we have, while we have it and respect this life and body for what it is, a temporal loan.

If we see it, for what it is, we will maintain focus on what matters the most. We will not lose focus because it is all or nothing and this is not our game. This earth, our very lives is simply not in our ball court and, so we must stop trying to dominate and learn to play by the rules. Get back to the book, the directions, and the roadmap for this temporal walk.

Hope you will read it, (The Bible) for it (He) is the only way home. Also, remember there is nothing wrong with giving it all up. All of my life I had to win. I played on my terms. Suddenly, when I was drowning and found I could not hold my head above water. When I found myself in a place where I was barely able to catch my breath; where It seemed as soon as I lifted my head above water that I was seemingly dunked back under again and again and I finally gave up and reached up, I found, I had been looking and living down. I was depending on my resources and me, which is so limited. However, when I gave it all up, and gained focus on whose really in control and decided to let him be lord, I gained more than I ever thought I could have. Even my thinking was limited compared to what he wanted to give to me.

In this, I came to a revelation, what wise parent would continually give presents to a child, who does not know how to appreciate a gift. Jesus is the Gift.

My house now is more than I had dreamt of. I received a better car than I had before. I was searching Craig's list for used furniture, but God said oh not so and gave me exceedingly, abundantly above all I could have dreamed or imagined. My choice of furniture on the showroom floor, paid in full, no financing necessary. Even gave me my baby boy who is the mirror image of my daughter that passed. I often remind him that he gets kisses for two, for you and my Tina, who looked and acted just as you do. God gave me back double for all that trouble Satan had put me through. Even in this now so-called recession I was not recessed but rather exceedingly blessed. Lending and not borrowing, handling life's business with supreme ease.

Everything belongs to God and he can give his gifts to whomsoever he pleases, or who pleases him. He said, seek ye first the kingdom of heaven and all else will be added. Every day when I wake up and look around me, I see his word in action because I'm living in his promise. I can tell you, he ain't ever lied, try him, and see for yourself.

Scriptures state St Luke (9:23-25) And he said to them all, "If any man will come after me, let him deny himself, and take up his cross daily and follow me. 24) For who so ever will save his life shall lose it, but whosoever will lose his life for my sake; the same shall save it. 25) For what is a man advantaged, if he gains the whole world, and lose himself, or be cast away?"

St Luke (9:62) states, "And Jesus said unto him, no man, having put his hand to the plough, and looking back, is fit for the kingdom of God." St Matt (10:37-38) He that loveth father or mother more than me is not worthy of me, and he that loveth son or daughter more than me is not worthy of me. 38) And he that taketh not his cross, and followeth after me, is not worthy of me.

Remember Jesus told the rich man go and sell all that you have or give it to the poor and follow me. It is, all or nothing. It doesn't belong to us anyway, so what do we have to lose but our Souls. Jesus didn't come to earth to gain possessions, he came to gain souls and he gave it all up. Remember he said, no man taketh my life but he laid it down freely for us.

He is the Gift. If we really understood and cherished the Gift, we will not have to worry about the gifts. For he promised, they will all be added onto us. St Luke (12:31) Seek ye first---first the kingdom of heaven and all else will be added.

Remember not some but all else that you need, he promised will be added unto you. He is worthy of his word. He placed his life on it. It's time for Christians to start living as if they were born to die, it's time for a radical change, in Jesus name.

Jannette Williams- Holt

True Love Is Tough

Although we may sometimes feel like God has turned his back on us, God is always here. He said, "I will never leave you nor forsake you." He said, "I love you with an everlasting love." Nothing that you do can separate you from his love.

He died for you on your nerdy day, your ugly day, your stinky, smelly bad breath, ugliest hairdo day. He knows your emotional nakedness and he loves you. That is why he said come as you are. God loves us unconditionally. When he looks at us he doesn't see our faults, he sees his blood, his heart, his love. So even though circumstances might make you feel at times like you're forsaken, alone, unloved. In addition, Satan might infiltrate your mind with thoughts like; if God loved me, he would not have allowed this or that to happen.

Remember scripture states, (St John 11:5) "Now Jesus loved Martha and her sister, and Lazarus." (11:33) "He groaned in spirit and was troubled when he saw Mary and the Jews weeping" (11:35) states "Jesus wept" for Lazarus, but he allowed Lazarus to die because he knew he would raise him up. God allowed Jesus to die. God allowed Jesus to be crucified because he knew his death would raise us up.

Yeah, God sometimes permits our flesh to die because he knows it would raise us up spiritually. So even though it's sometimes hard to believe that a loving God is seeing what we're going through and just sitting, watching idly by, we must remember that God is supreme, infinite. We cannot judge him on our merits. Who is his equal? We cannot expect him to see things as we see things, no, we must bend, break, and change because God is spirit and changes not. We see through the flesh, but we must grow up and see as he sees, in the spirit. We must mature enough to know that sometimes love; loves enough, to let go and let grow and true love must be tough.

I learned this lesson in a very hard place. On July 26th, 2000 around 2 pm, I found myself walking around the nursing station, of the pediatric ICU. Back and forth I walked around, oblivious to everyone around me. This place in the open became my prayer closet.

While I couldn't go into that room where they were calling a code blue on my baby, I was going to remain as close to that place, as they would allow me to be. If the unit secretary hadn't told me that they would call security to have me removed, I would not have released my baby's clasp fist from my shirt.

I remember when we were transferring her to the ICU. She wouldn't allow them to put her on the stretcher. I had to hold her as an infant in my arms, with her head lying on my shoulder and walk her to the unit.

I don't want to begin, to imagine, what she might have felt, trying to pant for air. Gasping to pull in a breath, every couple of seconds. Tina was being carefully monitored as we walked into the unit. And I remember the nurse and respiratory therapist looking alarmed at the drastic drop in her oxygen saturation rate.

Immediately upon entering the ICU, we were bombarded with healthcare professionals, Cardiologists, pulmonologists, Oncologists, Respiratory Therapist, nurses, and other doctors, all looking panicky as her vital signs plummeted. I remember my baby barely able to talk, trying to reach up and hold onto me, as they unclasped her fist from my shirt and unfastened her legs from around my waist. She was saying no, no, no and crying mommy, mommy while reaching for me, as they ushered me out, so that they could attend to her with a heavy, tender chest and weaken knees, I walked down to the waiting room to pray. Those couple of hours waiting, was the longest hours of my life. I prayed like I had never prayed before, but later I found that my prayers were not for her, but rather for me. In fact, this was how I had been praying since she was diagnosed with cancer, and I wasn't even aware of it, until this day.

I was praying "Oh God, please have mercy on me. I can't live if I have to bury my baby. God, my heart is so heavy, so strained with pain that it's about to burst out of my chest. My throat felt dry; it felt as if a bulging knot of pain just stood there compressed in my throat, choking me, almost enabling me to swallow. It hurt just to breathe in and exhale out. I felt as if someone had wedged a butcher knife into my chest and was slowly twisting it, around and around. A mortal wound, that should have killed me, but instead, it was just mocking me.

My God, I can't do this, I can't, please God show up and show me that you are here. I couldn't recall when it happened, but all I know, is that I fell into a deep sleep, trance-like, and when I woke up it was almost six hours later.

For the life of me, I don't know where the time went. I arrived at the ICU waiting room around 6 am, all I could tell you is that this was not a time that I would sleep. I remember seeing a white dove flying away, and I saw a clock that showed the small arm on 3 o'clock, and then someone tapped me on my shoulders, saying Mrs. Williams, do you have anyone with you? Straightaway I looked down at my watch and saw that it was after 2 pm. I don't know what happened in between what seemed like mere minutes.

I immediately said, where is my baby, can I see her? The person tapping me introduced themselves as the hospital Chaplin and a social worker, the last people you'd want to see together in the hospital. I didn't want to see them or hear anything they had to say. I knew that they were often sent as counselors, the bearers of bad news to the bereaving families. I wasn't ready to be considered the bereaved. Just let me see my baby, I said. Immediately someone answered, Mrs. Williams, is there anyone you would like for us to call? And with that, I started racing towards the ICU.

As I entered the unit and headed towards my baby's room someone stopped me. I just got to peep into Tina's room, which was still filled with doctors, nurses, and therapist, trying to resuscitate her. I heard one of the older doctors say, " Is that the mother?" as I was being pushed out of the room and back into the hallway.

A few minutes later, the primary doctor came out to talk to me; he said: "Mrs. Williams, am going to be honest with you, there is not much more that we can do for her." We've done everything within our power. We've been resuscitating her just about every hour, on the hour. I couldn't hear anything else he was saying; I just saw his mouth moving. Yet I knew, he was proposing my letting her go.

I remember saying no, I can't do that. Am consulting with another doctor. I must hear what he has to say. I wasn't trying to sound spiritual. God is all I had. God is all I got. He said what other doctor? I said, my God. He said okay, we'll continue the code. I thank God for his gentle spirit. He knew, that I was not ready, and he did not impose his professional directive on me.

About ten minutes later, he called me into her room, to see her. And while I know my baby, I could barely recognize her. Tina was lying there, paralyzed with drugs. Her eyes were taped shut. She seemed to have I. V's everywhere, in both of her feet, arms, and hands. She was topless, and her whole body appeared bloated with air and fluid. A drastic change from how I left her six hours earlier.

I left her looking weak and malnourished, from the effects of chemotherapy and radiation treatments but I returned to find her swollen from head to toe. And instead of her being on one ventilator to supplement her breathing, she was intubated and connected to two ventilators. Never had I seen anything like this before. Still, with all those tubing's, I wanted her to know that I was there. So, I picked her limp, flaccid body up into my arms and rested her head on my shoulder. I tightly squeezed and cuddled her small frame next to my chest

.

When I looked down into her puffy face, I remember seeing dry tears on her cheeks, and instantly my heart burst and changed, my prayers changed as well. Instead of focusing on me and my pain, I started thinking about her and her pain and about how selfish I had been. I started thinking about how miserable it must have been for her, sifting for air and barely able to breathe but still trying to hang on for me. And I was hurting even more now because I realized, while I thought I loved her, I was loving me more.

Just then I heard all the alarms on the monitor going off and I looked up to see her vital signs plummeting down. An army of hospital staff raced into the room and of course, ushered me out.

As I walked back into the hallway, I swear I don't remember seeing anyone else. There was this faint sound of murmuring around me, but soon, all I heard was me talking to God. I remember a shadow coming towards me and with tear-filled eyes and a heavy heart and chest I remembered just stretching forth my finger and motioning not now. Instantly, everything went black, as I prayed a prayer, I never dreamed I would pray.

Instead of continuing to pray God have mercy on me. I prayed God have mercy on her, with all my heart, I want her to live. I want her to grow strong and healthy. I want her to have an earthly future. God, I want to see her grown, with kids of her own. I want her here with me. But more than that, I want her to be pain-free and comfortable. I want her to be able to breathe freely. I don't want her to just live; I want her to have a quality life. God, I want you to do whatever is best for her peace, for her comfort. God, please think of me. Give me strength with your decision, but have mercy on her. If death is where she would be free of pain and all this suffering, then give me the strength to let her be free.

Please God, give me the strength to accept whatever you decide. Less than a minute later, a doctor came out and said "Am sorry, we tried, there's nothing else we could do. We couldn't bring her back this time." Moreover, to my surprise, I felt peace like I had never felt before, and I did not scream, faint, or die like I thought I would.

I don't know where they came from, but instantly my dad, mom, sisters, and pastor were all around me. Immediately I knew that God had spoken, and I said, it is well with my soul. But God you know that I am human, so please help this to remain well with my soul. I asked God to please help me to stay content with him and his decision, because I honestly didn't know what to expect inwardly nor within the next hour or the days and nights ahead.

Feelings can be like a roller coaster. I needed God to stabilize my steps and my emotions and too not allow me to get it twisted when he came down to who I am and who he is.

My God, my Heavenly Father, I need you to walk with me because I don't' know how to do this? Please show and explain to me how to do this? I don't know how to walk out of this hospital and drive home alone, when my drive here every other day included her beside me in that passenger seat. God, I don't know how to leave her behind without looking back. So right now, I need you to walk with me. I need you to carry me because I don't even know how to steer this wheel, my feet feel too weak and wobbly to even press the gas. I Don't know how to start this engine or even in which direction to drive. I talked to God just like that, because right then, I was literally moving without knowing how to pick up my feet.

I don't remember what anyone was saying, but I felt good seeing friend and family. On July 26th, 2000 I learned, that love is not just holding on tight, but true love; loves enough, to let go and let grow. True love always considers the other person needs and holds their best interest at heart. God did this with Jesus when he sent him to die for us. He could have come down and instantly save Jesus, but where would that have left us, destined for Hell. Love must be tough and able to love enough to let go and let grow. God is Love. He let go of Jesus so that he can build and fill us up with his Holy Spirit.

When Joseph was stripped of his coat of many colors, sold into slavery, accused of assault by Pharaoh's wife and thrown into prison. God was there loving him, keeping him, and showing him favor with dreams and interpretation of dreams and prospering him even in prison, while raising him up. It was all a set-up, for a step up. Although he could not see it at that time, love was lifting him, inward and outwardly.

All that trouble was not only working together for his good but for the good of his father and brothers and many others that would be facing seven years of famine and needing someone humbled, Godly, and wise as overseer.

Sometimes God allows us to go through, remember the operative word, **through** a hard situation, or would harden a Pharaohs' heart so that we will not only come out but also come out exceedingly, abundantly above all we can think, dream, or imagine.

In addition, no matter how dark it seems, remember, God works in ways we cannot see. Trust in his love. In (Second Kings 6:16-17) when Elisha was running from the king of Syria, was surrounded by the Syrian army and his servant cried out to him in fear.

God in love, allowed Elisha to see into the supernatural. Elisha, in turn, was able to say to his servant 16) "Don't be afraid!" Elisha told him. "For our army is bigger than theirs!" Some things only spiritual eyes can see. Ooh, but remember love never fails. Things are always happening behind the scenes that natural eyes are not permitted to see but God is love, and he changes not. 17) Then Elisha prayed, "Lord, open his eyes and let him see!" And the Lord opened the young man's eyes so that he could see horses of fire and chariots of fire everywhere upon the mountain!" (Second Kings 6:16-17 The Catholic Living Bible) Elisha knew to trust in God's love because earlier in scripture Elisha got to witness Gods walking with Elijah, fellowshipping with him. Scripture states, 11) "As they were walking along, talking, suddenly a chariot of fire, drawn by horses of fire, appeared and drove between them, separating them, and Elijah was carried by a whirlwind into heaven." (Second Kings 2:11 The Living Bible) God so loved Elijah's fellowshipping, friendship, sonship that like Enoch, he did not even allow him to taste the sting of death. In splendor, he sent a special escort to take him home to glory.

You know, God loves us just the seam. Although we can't see it, we're all transported to heaven as princess and prince. God sends his angels to take our spirit into eternity the instant we die. (For scripture tells us to be absent from the body, is to be present with the lord.) He separates our eternal spirits from these earthen vessels, these jars of clay and ushers us into glory. Not only does love never to fail, sometimes love goes out of the way showering us with splendor.

In love, in love, God swung open the gates of heaven, allowing Stephen to look up and look in. Letting him know without words, do not be afraid, because I am with you. He allowed him to go deep into the spirit, so that he could see the recent crucified and resurrected Jesus at his right hand. Letting him know, not only are you not alone, but you are in good company. Like Jesus, Stephen was able to say. "Father into thine hand I commit my spirit." In the presence of pure unadulterated love, he was able to look beyond in love as well and say, "Lord lay not this sin to their charge". And when he had said that he fell asleep.

Moreover, remember, no matter how dark the night might be, even if death shall step in, you have to know, that you will still see the real Son in the morning. The love that lights up this world, the bright and morning star. Nothing can ever separate us from him.

Remember, God did not just allow Shadrach, Meshach, and Abednego to be thrown into that fiery furnace but in love, he went in with them. Ministering to them and keeping their company.

Scripture said Nebuchadnezzar was so angry regarding them not bowing to his gods that he commanded the furnace be turned up seven times hotter. He commanded his strongest men to bound them. Because his command was so urgent, the furnace was exceedingly hot. So hot that the flames of the fire slew those men that threw Meshach, Shadrach, and Abednego into the fire. Yet, although they fell bond amid the fire, upon their bodies the fire had no power, nor was their hair or head singed, neither was their coats changed, nor had the smell of fire passed on them.

In the presence of Almighty God even the elements, fire and wind know to behave. "Nebuchadnezzar astonished raised up and spoke unto his counselor saying, "Did not we cast three men bond into the midst of the fire, they answered, 'True king "He, Nebuchadnezzar answered, lo, I see four men loose, walking in the midst of the fire and they have no hurt, and the form of the fourth is like the son of God." (Daniel 3:24) There is a powerful message here, hope you got it. They were walking amid the fire with no hurt because they maintained focus. Their eyes were not on the fire but on the helper.

God is love. Moreover, in his infinite wisdom, he created us with this empty, vacant place. This longing for fulfillment in each of us that can only be filled by his presence, his love, not the love of another human being or earthly things. It is a vacancy for his Holy Spirit to enter in and fill. Like a jigsaw puzzle, only perfect pieces fit to bring it together completed, counterfeit parts will not be substituted. He said in scripture that he was going away but that he will send us a comforter, our holy completion. When Adam ate the forbidden fruit, he robbed us of that completion, but ----Jesus came and died on the cross so that he could dwell with and in us again, here on earth.

In addition, anyone who asks shall receive him. Love is gentle he will not force himself on us. Love is the truth; it will lead us into all truth. Love is patient and kind; it will create in us a clean heart. When the comforter comes (got that, the comforter, the peace, the lover, sustainer, strengthener, guide) comes, old things will slowly start passing away, as he grows us up into a new creation, resembling him.

Love never ever fails. Therefore, God never ever fails, for scriptures say God is love. Scripture states, "Love covereth all sins" (Proverb 10.12) God loves Shedrach, Meshach and Abednego, God loves Stephen, Elijah, Elisha, Joseph and you, but God said as many as I love, I rebuke. (Rev 3:19) Love must be tough, or we'd all end up in hell. We have to be disciplined and corrected, brought up to holiness.

As his children, we must be obedient and allow him to be our father. Allow him to grow us up into his image, into Christ-likeness. We have to be redirected, in order to not succumb to this flesh. God sees where our path will lead us. So, as a loving, stern father, who has much more wisdom and hindsight then we do, he has to discipline us in order to uphold us.

Nevertheless, remember no matter what happens he is on your side. For in (Romans 8:35-39) scriptures states. "Who shall separate us from the love of Christ? Shall tribulations, or distress, or perils, or swords or famine or nakedness 36) as it is written; for thy sake, we are killed all the day long, we are considered as sheep for the slaughter. 37) Nay, in all these things, we are more than conquerors through him that loved us. 38) For I am persuaded, that neither death, nor life, nor angel, nor principalities, nor powers, nor things present, nor things to come. (Meaning no matter what, we are covered) 39) nor height, nor depth, nor any other creature, shall be able to separate us from the love of God, which is in Christ Jesus our Lord."

Remember Scripture states. Love never fails. 13) "And now these three remain; faith, hope, and love. But the greatest of these is love." (First Corinthians 13:8&13 NIV) God is love, so again if love never fails, then know this, that God never fails. Lean on his strong shoulders, he is able to carry your weight.

It's Still All or Nothing

It's Still All or Nothing

The Good Shepherd
Never Forgets His Sheep

When my mom and daughter died, I truly learned what it meant to have God as my Shepherd. People probably thought it strange or even stupid of me because I did not, could not cry at my mom's or daughters homegoing services. However, what nobody else knew, God knows. As soon as I received the message of their passing before I allowed myself to get caught up in me, into my humanness, into blaming and questioning or cursing God. I knew I had to give it over to him because I was now in a place I had never been in before.

Moreover, I learned a long time ago, when lost, seek direction. Therefore, I lifted my voice and heart and I praised God in truth as never before, for his sovereignty. Thanking him for his perfect will and for his blessings. I asked him to take complete control of my mind, heart and being. I asked him to keep me sober-minded, even-tempered, and self-controlled. I asked him to keep me focus on him, and absolutely not on me. Before my loss could sink in, I got lost in the spirit. And God in his love and faithfulness kept me wrapped up, clasped, tightly cuddled in his presence, in his spirit, until I was strong enough to stand on my own.

Being amid my sisters and family and seeing them mourn, I felt as if I should be bawling and caring on as well. However, I could not feel sad, loss, sorrow, or death. In fact, I felt the presence of life more than I ever had before. No one can come into his presence and feel darkness and death, for he is life; he is light.

Two of the most important people in my life were no longer with me. Physically, I would never hear their voice again. I would never be able to touch, hold or be in their company again. Yet, instead of feeling loss, I felt a high that nothing on earth could compare too. The peace and joy I felt no man, drug or anything on earth could counterfeit or duplicate. Inside I knew that God was carrying me. Only those who felt that heavenly peace will understand what I am talking about. Believe me, if you did not know and you felt it, you will know beyond any doubt, even if you never read another word in the Bible, that he is real.

When my baby died, I slept like a baby. People came to lend their support and comfort. To offer their condolence but God spoke to my spirit and said because you fully trust me, I'm going to be your comforter. I rolled my burdens on God, and it was as if God waved his hand over me and put me into a deep, peaceful sleep.

Although I was fighting with every fiber of my being to stay awake and show appreciation for my support, my eyes were too heavy for me to keep open. I could not understand it. I never slept so peaceful before or after that night. It was as if I had been temporarily transformed into another realm; rather than merely asleep.

Sometimes we must endure a little sorrow or allot of sorrow so that a bigger plan can be fulfilled, a more meaningful purpose. And although you can only see vaguely now, you will understand the bigger plan for this season later.

Do know that Kristina not being physically healed was not me forsaking you. God took me to heaven where Kristina was and said to me, although you guys are saddened down there, up here a celebration is going on that no celebration on earth could compare too.

He opened my eyes and I saw broad, giant men, twelve to fifteen feet tall and miniature dwarfs three feet tall singing, marching, dancing, blowing trumpets, beating drums, and performing with instruments that I could not even name. I mean heaven was having a fabulous, indescribable parade, carrying Tina high up in the air, as if she was a princess. The singing was the most beautiful singing I have ever heard, words that no lyrist on earth could write music too. Words that no composer down here can write a tune too.

In addition, the clothing I cannot even describe, it was so beautiful. And love just exuded like osmosis, like electricity through the atmosphere, through every being. I felt God spirit wrapped all around me. I felt like I was floating. Days after I woke up, I still felt as if I was gliding around. Again, I knew that God was carrying me. I was hearing music, songs that I had forgotten the words too I was hearing songs that I had not heard since I was a child in Sunday School. Now I believe I know what the scripture means by out of your belly shall flow rivers of living water. A life, loving, peaceful stream, flowing, saturating my every fiber.

At a time when I was supposed to be the saddest, I could not help but sing. In my spirit, everywhere I went, in the bathroom, around the house, in the car, those songs brought such peace and joy that I had to verbally express what was springing up inside of me. David says God inhabits our praise, (Ps 22:3) meaning he comes in and dwells in, occupies, lives in, takes up residence, lingers in our praise and where the spirit of the lord is, there is liberty. (Second Corinthians 3:17) Absolutely nothing on earth like his presence, that is why David said take not from me thy presence. (Ps 51:11) If you felt it, you know. I now understand why he told Joshua and the Israelite children to just walk around the wall of Jericho singing. Sometimes, sometimes, a song is all we need to usher him in, and when he is in, it is a done deal. It is finished. The battle is over. Remember Jehoshaphat went in with praise and worship and confused the enemy. (Second Chronicles 20:15- 24)

I also understand why, when Paul and Silas forgot about their circumstances in prison and just rested in praise and worship the earth quaked and the prison bars flew open; for what can possibly tie God down or imprison him. How did the church get away from lingering in worship, from lingering in his presence? For one minute in his presence outweighs an hour of preaching. Why, when in church, do we not usher him in and just let him, let Pentecost, let the Holy Spirit have its way? We need his fire and he knew we would, that is why he instructed us to wait on him. We must let him lead, for he will always be the Shepherd and we the sheep.

In God's presence is joy unspeakable and fullness of grace, amazing grace. God also told me that he was going to take this burden off my heart and that he was going to send helpers; physical helpers. At that time, I did not know how this would manifest but I did know that on the day that Tina died, although I did not know how I was going bury her. I knew in my heart that just as I am Gods business, everything in my life, and about my life, including this, was Gods business and he would take care of it. I knew, that I knew, that I knew, even without a penny that God had everything under control. No, did not sit saying prayers about it, I just cast it over to him, and knew he had it handled.

I had no life insurance policy, no job, no savings, or checking account. I had nothing, just my breath, my life, and my sincere praise. However, God sent helpers just as he said, from everywhere. Someone donated a free burial plot, someone I still do not know because it was anonymous. When I went to the funeral home to pay for her embalming I was told it was already taken cared of by my pastor. A burial vault was anonymously donated. Miami Children Hospital gave a two-thousand-dollar check. Checks and cash were given from people, some of whom I had never met or known.

Mind you, I never published my needs, just was ever mindful that God still holds everything, so he can freely release anything. When everything was calculated, I had enough money to pay in full for Kristina funeral service, leaving money over to help me get back on my feet.

Not only did God send full provision for Tina's service. Remember God is God, he does not do anything halfway. When he is doing the catering, or furnishing the event he outdoes all we could think or dream of.

Instead of Tina just having one wake, he fully funded two wakes, with more than enough food and drinks then we could eat. Believe me, when we truly trust God to take over, he goes all out. I had brand-new clothes for Tina and both of my other kids during her service, after her service I was able to give money away. Ask me about exceedingly, abundantly above all we could think, dream, or imagine. I know. I can tell you from nothing to giving, without a penny, but God.

Yes, he is not only able but also willing, and if you trust him, he will take care of you. For he is the good Shepherd that goeth out before the sheep preparing the way and making the crooked places straight. Just as his word says, he is faithful.

Therefore, if ever, you are feeling forsaken or alone, think back on the lilies, on how he so clothe them. Remember he said in (St Luke 12: 27- 28) Remember, "If then God so clothe the grass, which today is in the field and tomorrow is thrown into the oven, how much more will he clothe you. 27) Consider the Lillie's (really consider them) how they grow, they neither toil nor spin; and yet I say to you even Solomon in all of his glory was not arrayed like one of these." He also said in (St Luke, 12:24) "Consider the ravens, for they neither sow nor reap, which have neither storehouses nor barn; and God feedeth them; (Of how much more value are you than the birds?) How much more are ye better than the fowls?"

God does not just say things to make noise, he said them so that we would really hear and not only hear but trust and know that he is concerned about us. His words are meant to build our confidence in him.

He stated these parables to re-emphasize to us that we are covered. That he holds our future, and to assure us that he will meet our every need. Moreover, to remind us to get our minds off our circumstances and keep our eyes on him. If we as the sheep stay in line behind the Shepherd, we would always end up in safe pastures. Too often we try to run ahead, we want to lead, because we can't wait to arrive. Yet we are not as strong as he is, we have not traveled these roads before and he has. We do not have all the necessary resources and he has more than enough.

If only we would stay under the covering, no matter what, then we like the three Hebrew boys and Daniel in the lion's den will come out not even smelling of smoke; and with the lions protecting us instead of attacking us.

If he is our covering, then everything must go through him, to get to us. David says (Ps 37:24-25) "Though he fall, he shall not be utterly cast down; for the Lord upholdeth him with his hand. I have been young, and now I am old; yet have I not seen the righteous forsaken, nor their seed begging bread."

Yes, God is still the Good Shepherd who would leave the ninety and nine just for the love of you. Just remain the sheep and let him be Sheppard until you have finished your race and can one day open your eyes in his presence, knowing that the great commission was fulfilled through your living, for our king and the kingdom. Knowing that you did not come home empty-handed, nor did you hide your talents like the wick evil servant but, like Paul proudly saying and knowing, "I have fought the good fight."

No Test
Beyond His Sovereignty

We are predestined. This life, our breath, our being is not perchance. God did not just make anyone or anything. He knew what he was fashioning together when he created you and me. God knows what is in you. However, God wants you to know what is in you. He wants us to see that this mess that we call Christianity in our lives, is not okay. Even a little sin, a little compromising, is not Christ-like. So sometimes he has to allow us to break, so that we may see the cracks. Because the cracks are where sin and Satan are able to enter in. We can't afford to leave any room for Satan; if we can help it and if Gods Holy Spirit dwells within us, we have the power to help it.

We are fighting against spiritual forces in high places, against principalities and the rulers of darkness of this world; and they are not playing, so God is not playing. (check out the inner cities, remember Columbine and Virginia Tech.) We have to be refined, made strong, steadfast, and immovable, in order to withstand these forces. Remember, Jesus came into the world so that we may have life and life more abundantly.

However, the adversary has come to kill, steal, and destroy. (John 10:10) So every chance he gets he is going to try to tempt and detour you. Remember scriptures states "Let no man when he is tempted say I am tempted of God, for God cannot be tempted with evil, neither tempteth he any man; but every man is tempted when he is drawn away of his own lust, and enticed." We are drawn away by our own evil desires when we take our eyes off God. God is not willing, but God permits Satan tempting when we broke down the hedge and allow the enemy to come in.

I helped create some of my own wilderness, but thanks be to God, whether through our own doing or through Satan's sending; until our true destiny is fulfilled there will be test in our lives that we are destined to win. Some test of our own hard-headedness can literally take us through hell.

As an example, when I was nineteen years old I went to visit the Turks and Caicos Islands. There I met this guy name Trent, with whom I became instant best friends. Trent was not rich, but unbeknownst to me, in one week he swept me off my feet. We met at a beach splash down, where we played kickball on the sand with some of my cousins. Trent and my cousin Jada were friends. Although I saw him, he was far from my thoughts, because I assumed he had something going on with Jada. Me, my cousins and Trent, made plans to meet later that night, at this club called the Banana Boat, where my cousin Blake and his band would be performing.

Around nine o'clock that night as planned, approximately ten to fifteen of us tried to hop on the back of this pickup truck. We were all cousins' two truckloads full, laughing and making jokes, unbeknownst to me, building precious lasting memories. Suddenly, we turned around a curb and a few of us almost fell off the truck, just then Trent came up on his motorcycle and Jada started climbing down to ride with him, but then he said: "Jada, let your cousin ride with me." She said, "Netty he is crazy as hell, but he's cool, do you want to ride with him?" I said sure. I didn't mind because I was looking forward to having an adventure, and a motorcycle was a cool way of zipping around in the Island breeze. Besides, on this small island, everyone knew everyone.

As we drove around the narrow-curved street of Blue Hills, I was pleased with my decision, it was so beautiful riding around Providenciales at night. I remember Trent was playing this song called "Oh Baby I Love Your Way," which not only had a nice beat to it but also fit right into that Island vibe. Me and Trent started singing in sync with each other. We hit it off right away, I felt calm and undisturbed, as if we had known each other all of our lives. We went to visit some of his friends, where we sat down and talked for a while, then we drove onto the Banana Boat where it felt like a family event. Although there were a lot of tourist and other island natives there, whom I did not know, I had cousins present from wall to wall and it felt like a big family reunion, rather than a local nightclub.

My cousin Blake surprisingly dedicated a song to me, his cousin Netty, who was visiting from Miami. Which Immediately brought a few of my other cousins and old friends whom I hadn't seen in years, running towards me. We instantly hugged each other and started jumping around embraced in a big circle, screaming as if we'd lost our minds; being crazy teenagers and young adults.

Later, Trent said to me, "Netty, come ride with me, there is this other hot spot that you just have to see." I was excited to explore and enjoy all that Turks Islands had to offer. So, we jumped on his bike and went club hopping. He took me to see this area called South Dock, that was supposed to be one of the prettiest parts of the island at night.

As we parked the bike, a song came on the radio by Journey, and then another song by Air Supply and instantly we both started singing at the top of our lungs, as if we didn't have a care in the world. We were surprised that we both knew all the words. Straight away, we started battling each other to see how many of their songs we both knew. We had belly-aching laughs as we did some of their songs absolutely, no justice, improvising to beat the battle and often catching each other jumbling up on the words. All this time I wasn't even thinking of him as a possible boyfriend because I was only visiting for a week, and I had a boyfriend back home.

Around four o'clock we went to Club Le Deck, where we met up with some more of my cousins. Finally, still club hopping, in this very young, beautiful night, we ended up at a Club MED where we sat on one of the most beautiful beaches in the Turks and Caicos Islands. We drank a few kailiks while relaxing in the beautiful lights of the homes in the distance, which seemed to encircle the aqua blue waters within them. We made jokes and talked on and on about life. I got home around six in the morning, filled and exhausted.

About seven thirty, just when I was about completely knocked out, I heard loud banging on my bedroom window. I immediately placed a pillow over my head to drown out the noise. I had no idea who that was and I really didn't care, but the banging would not stop. I screamed out, please whoever you are just go away. Still, the banging would not stop. Furiously, I threw the pillow to the side and raced over to the window, opening the curtains to see Trent, grinning in my face. I could have whopped his butt with my bare hands.

Wasn't the both of us up all night, I thought. What the hell! Shouldn't you be at home asleep? Nooo, he decided he was coming to take me to breakfast. I retorted am not a breakfast person, come back around dinner time. But grinning and absolutely pissing me off, he decided that he was not going to stop banging until I got dressed and joined him because he was not going to eat alone. I got up and got dressed, but not to join him, but rather to beat this hell out of him.

I asked Trent to go on ahead of me, told him that I will meet him at Mr. Joe's restaurant in about fifteen minutes. He turned and cautioned me that if I did not show up within twenty minutes, he will be back. When I arrived at the restaurant I remember him sitting there trying to look cool, smoking a cigarette. He asked what do I want to order and I sternly stated not one damn thing. See these tennis shoes I have on when you get through eating I have something for you. He started laughing hysterically, my lips never swayed, neither did my eyes. I was serious as hell. Oh! he said, you actually look like you think you could take me. I replied, what would make you think, I can't? Trent started laughing hysterically again and stated, "Take me! You and what army?" I don't need an army, I said, I got you. Trent stayed in the restaurant and played with his food a little longer than he should have.

I later learned that he thought to himself that although I was small, I might have a black belt in karate or something and he didn't want to embarrass himself.

He asked me to meet him for dinner later that day and I instantly decided that I wasn't going. Instead, I took a boat ride with some friends to this private island called Water Key, where we chased Iguanas and picnicked for the day. When I got back home, my aunt Mary told me that some guy on a motorcycle came by a couple of times looking for me.

I thought he was a little persistent. Right after I cleaned up, he called on the phone asking me to meet him at the airport. And I thought, for what! What kind of restaurant is at the airport? So, I didn't even think twice about going. That next day I hung out riding around the island, listening to music and drinking beers with my cousin Blake. When I got home, he was at it again, after several phone calls, I decided to meet up with him.

When I reached the airport he was outside waiting for me and instead of going into the airport restaurant to eat, he led me straight pass the reservationist, straight through customs, straight through the airport security an onto the tarmac. Where we boarded this little six-seater plane that was gearing up in the distance, and am thinking okay. What is this? To my surprise, after we stepped up onto the aircraft, where an older Caucasian couple was sitting, the pilot closed the door and we started gliding down the tarmac.

Trent decided he was going to show me some of the other Cays in the Turks and Caicos Islands. First, we stopped off at West Caicos than South Caicos, Middle Caicos, Grand Turk and finally North Caicos, his hometown, where we went to this little family-owned restaurant and I ate some of the most finger-licking crab and rice, baked Marconi and cheese and steamed chicken I have ever tasted.

My mouth was still tingling hours after with the sting of those tantalizing juices and pungent flavors. Later that night we went to this little area name Kew where he grew up, there I met his family and friends. Everybody knew each other in Kew and that night I saw the genuine meaning of friendship and neighbor, as I watched this community come together. One of the young men from Kew left for one of the neighboring islands to work and had been in a horrific car accident, apparently just clinging to life.

He had to be flown out to one of the bigger Caribbean hospitals for critical care treatment. That night, it seemed the whole town stayed up, sitting on this wall next to his family home, keeping their company, while awaiting word on his condition. I was so impressed with that sincere assembly of togetherness.

On the other hand, what really changed my mind towards Trent was that next day when we went to this nearby town called Whitby. There we ate lunch and then we stopped by the beach and spend the remainder of that day with his friend Lonnie. Trent and Lonnie played their guitars, smoked weed and sung reggae and calypso songs while talking nonsense about the meaning of life, until the sun went down. All in all, this was one of the most beautiful, just relax and do-nothing days of my life. Both Trent and Lonnie were lead singers in different bands on the Islands and in my opinion, both could have given Bob Marley a run for his money, with his own songs, on any given day. It was like having my very own, private reggae concert, on the beach, all evening long.

On our way back to Kew, we were talking and laughing and I thought still having a good time; although we couldn't see anything before or behind us because there were no street lights. We couldn't even see our teeth in this thick darkness. Suddenly, Trent became completely, unnaturally quiet as I continued to talk, but I didn't think anything of it. Suddenly he said, do me a favor and take off your shoes, and hold them in your hands. Again, I thought, what! Why! Trent said, just trust me and follow my lead.

No sooner than I had my shoes off, I felt something or someone zip pass me. It felt like the wind and I heard him up ahead, in the distance screaming at the top of his lungs. I don't know what triggered that response from him, but I remember my soon passing him. I use to run track in school. Whatever, in hell, we were running from, I would have to find out about later. Although I was the stranger to these roads, he would have to meet me wherever we were headed.

About fifteen minutes later, I saw the glare of vehicle lights behind in the distance and I didn't hear Trent screaming or running anymore. I immediately looked back and saw that he had slowed down and was talking to the people in the truck. He called out to me to come back, and we both jumped on the back of the truck for the rest of the ride into Kew. After I caught my breath I asked him, what the hell was that?

He started laughing hysterically and said that we were walking past one of the oldest graveyards on the islands. "I know I heard someone whistling, he said, that's why I stopped talking, to be sure, and sure enough, there was whistling." Trent said, "Sorry, but some of these people are older than my grandparents, grandparents and I am not trying to meet any of them." "I don't care to see no Jumbees." (That's what they call spirits or ghost in the islands) We were both bent over with bellyaching laughter as I made fun, back, and forth, mimicking the way he was running and screaming. That next morning we took a boat along with his brother and sister in law back to Provo. We spent that night hanging around my cousins' house, sitting on the wall, drinking Kaliks and making jokes.

That next day I was packed and headed back to Miami. Trent met me at the airport and begged me not to go back. He started crying, talking about how much he was going to miss me and I thought he was crazy. We had only known each other for a few days, actually less than a week. So I said goodbye and headed back to Florida. I thought I was in love before, but I realized a few days later, that unbeknown to me, I had fallen and fallen hard.

I later recognized, that we don't even realize when we're having the time of our lives until it's over. I had this pain in my chest and I couldn't figure out how it got there, but I knew why. Boy did my heart ache for his company. This misery was so new to me. I realized much later what he must have been feeling, when he begged me to stay.

I now realized, that I had had, the time of my life, with my best friend of only a few days. A month later I moved back to the islands and I don't know how he knew I was coming because we had not stayed in contact, but when I came through customs there he was waving me over to him.

Although I had bags, I still jumped on the back of his motorcycle and we followed the cab with my belongings to my aunt's house.

It's impossible to know someone in only a few days. Trent and I were hanging out together for breakfast, lunch, dinner, and snack; it was as if I never left.

This whole time, everywhere we went, people that I didn't even know was warning me about this young man I was keeping company with, but I didn't think anything of it. I thought I knew him, and I hadn't seen any bad sides to him yet.

This trip, I stayed in The Turks and Caicos Island for almost a year before heading back to Miami. Trent had gotten arrested for supposedly taking someone's property, he said he didn't do it and I believed him. God kept sending people to warn me that he was not for me. However, being in luuve! I could not see how he could not be. We were like peas in a pot, like white on rice, or so I thought. If Trent had any bad habits, there was no way, I thought! I could not have known. Nonetheless, he had been arrested and I moved back to Florida, believing in his innocence.

Three months later his sister called and asked me to meet her at her house, stating that she wanted to show me something. I was on my way to work, so I told her I would meet with her in the morning, but she insisted that what she wanted to show me couldn't wait until morning. She promised that it would only take a few minutes. So I decided that I would make a quick stop at her house.

She led me into her bedroom to show me a pair of new shoes she had bought, supposedly to ask my opinion on whether they were a good match, to an outfit she wanted to wear. As we were talking, Trent jumped out of her closet! Scaring me half to death, he picked me up off the ground and whirled me around and around. I was happy and surprised but I had to leave for work.

He decided that he waited too long for this day and that where ever I was going, he was going too. So he followed me along with his brother and some friends of theirs. They didn't mind staying in the waiting room where I worked, while I ran back and forth having small talk with them.

About two months later, without consulting God, we went to the local courthouse and got married. That's when all hell broke loose. Somehow, Trent was working every day but never getting paid. For some reason, his boss was always having problems with the bank and promising to pay him later. I would buy things and just know that I laid them down at a particular place in the house but for the life of me, those things would later be nowhere to be found. I almost thought that I was losing my mind.

First, it was little things like my earrings and bracelets; then the new bath towels and rugs, my new sweat suit, and finally the TV and stereo. People started coming around demanding money from me that he borrowed, in which I knew nothing about.

I suspected but did not want to believe that he was on drugs. I knew that I could compete with another woman, but drugs were a whole other ball game. And frankly, I didn't know how or where to even begin.

We sat down and had a talk in which I, unfortunately, found out that my suspicion was on point. Through my job, I got Trent into a drug rehab center, which cost us more than we could afford. I had to get a payroll deduction plan for the seventy-five dollars a day that I was responsible for paying. This program was supposed to be for twenty-one days, but Trent didn't even stay a week.

Trent later said that he was happy with his life and that he did not need to change. So, we separated for a while, then I decided that if we moved out of town, that if we had a change of environment and a change in friends that it might be better for him and subsequently for us.

Thus we moved to this little town called Lake Wales, where he immediately made a hand full of new friends of the vilest kind. Two weeks into our move, the landlord came tapping on the door stating that he needed his rent money by morning or we would have to leave. I was wondering what the hell he was talking about because I had personally paid him up front for the month's rent.

He stated that right after I placed the rent money in his hands, my husband came to talk with him, saying that we had a family emergency, and that he would need half of that money back but that we would make good on it by the week's end. Trent didn't have one brown cent, not even one brown penny, and I was thoroughly pissed off. I felt at ease thinking that I had a few dollars in the bank for emergencies that would cover this expense.

However, to my surprise, I don't know how he found it, but I guess I made it too obvious, my birthday being my pin number on my bank card. I got to the bank and wasn't able to withdraw anything, the ATM kept showing a zero balance. I was already late for work, so I decided that I would have to deal with this later. I worked the three to eleven thirty shift. When I got off from work a little past midnight and pulled up into our parking lot there were a gang of filthy looking,

Mexican migrant workers, apparently waiting for me. They bombarded my car, shaking it, while excitedly bidding me to get out.

Apparently, my husband, who was nowhere in sight, had made a deal offering me up to them. I felt dirty, cheap, and nauseated. I could not imagine being touched by these men. I sped out of that parking lot like a bat, on fire, out of hell. Almost, as soon as I pressed my feet on my gas paddled, I heard sirens blaring behind me. An Unsympathetic police officer, who did not even care to hear why I had been speeding and breathless, wrote me a ticket for two hundred and ninety-six dollars. For me this was the last straw, this relationship had tested every fiber of my being.

This relationship, in which God had sent warnings from every direction, bidding me to run. I could now see would eventually cost me my life, if I continued to stay. So, I started working on divorce proceedings.

I told Trent that I had done my best, but he had to want to change and since he said that his life was perfect, then for my safety I had to move on. Trent said he had gotten married until death do us part, and that, that would be my only way out. However, I could care less, the things I mentioned in this reading wasn't even the half of it. This relationship had literally become hell on earth.

I was finished and could care less if he saw me on the streets and acted as though he did not know me. In fact, he would have been doing me a favor by doing so. Rather, he started hanging around my job and harassing and threatening me. The security guard at my job had become my friend because he had to walk me from my car in the morning and back to my car at night. Trent said to me, "Do you think him walking you around mean anything to me, he can't stop me, even God can't arrest me."

I took his declaration with a grain of salt, until a few days later when I was headed towards my car to go to work. Out of nowhere, Trent came dashing towards me, with a big butcher knife. I screamed at the top of my lungs while tussling with him from side to side, struggling for my life.
As small as my apartment complex was, it seemed as if no one could hear me. Soon I realized that in this life, people readily close their ears and turn the other way, so long as they're not directly affected. This makes me wonder about people whose lives could have been saved if all neighbors were indeed fellow citizens. What harm is there in anonymously dialing 911?

After what seemed like an eternity, I heard a gunfire into the air and one of my neighbors, Mrs. Patty came running outside in her nightgown, shouting, "You better leave because the cops are on their way!"

Trent totally marginalized her, I couldn't believe it. His mission had been to end my life that day. He continued to tussle with me while screaming back at her that this was none of her business. Mrs. Patty shouted back, "Yes this is my business." "I have daughters her age and I refuse to turn away, not on my watch!" Suddenly, I heard the police siren in the distance. Still, he did not budge. Police cars surrounded the parking lot on every side and I heard them tell him to drop the knife, or they will shoot. It seemed like forever before he dropped it.

After the police freed me and placed him in the police car, all I wanted to do was go home; not to my apartment upstairs but truly home, back to where my mom lived. However, the police told me that I needed to stay because they needed to get a statement from me. I could not understand, how a love that seemed so right, so perfect, could turn out to be so flawed.

One police officer came over to where I was sitting, on the lower stairway, and literally shaking, as if I was in a freezer, and actually had the nerve to ask me, do I want to talk to him. Because he said he wanted to say something to me before they took him off to jail. I didn't answer, I just gave him a look that said, are you serious!!

After what seemed like an unnecessarily long time, the police finally told me that I could leave. Still trembling, I got into my car. I was barely able to hold my hands still enough, to place my keys in the ignition.

In a daze and still jittery I drove to my mom's house. I had a key and it was still early in the morning, so I just went inside and climbed my grown twenty-something behind into her bed and cuddled as close as I could right up under her. Because that was home to me. There I knew I was loved and understood.

I was still quivering, because I kept seeing myself laid out on the ground, with a white sheet covering my frame. I was weak and exhausted. I just knew that if Mrs. Patty hadn't stepped in when she did, that I would have been a corpse, through this bed that I helped to make, in hell.

A few minutes after my arrival, my mom jumped up and said, "Net, what's wrong?" "You're shaking as if you just saw a ghost." Yeah, I thought, I was that ghost. I was still in shock, I couldn't even talk.

Yet! I couldn't ask God why he had forsaken me, or why had he allowed me to go through such hell in this relationship. I couldn't ask God how someone who said they loved me, someone who said he would take a bullet for me on any given day, would hate me so much that he would want to see me dead. I couldn't ask God why, because he had been sending people out of the woodworks just to tell me, that I was on the wrong path.

Don't misunderstand me, the Trent I truly know, has one of the biggest hearts God has ever created. Drugs are the force here, that stole, killed and destroyed. Anyone who truly knows Trent, before the drugs, will tell you that he will give his last to even a stranger. He will start making jokes in response to harsh words in order to change the atmosphere. He would easily give up his right, rather than retaliate and add combustion to an argument. He genuinely love people. He is one of those people who truly never met a stranger. But that devil is eviler than hell. He is hell. But he ain't bigger than God.

However, this one was on me. I did this to myself. I decided that my heart would not lead me wrong, but my heart and my stubborn, know it all flesh, almost led me to the grave. All this time in my life, although I grew up in church, I had God on the back burner. And I was happy, I thought, living my life. From a young age I was told that I had a calling on my life. But for now, I was young. I just started living and like Nebucanezzar my life was all about me. Yet, there are tests that we are destined to win because when we are called or chosen, no devil in hell can take us out. Jesus slipped right through the Pharisees, right through the crowd. Saying, my time has not yet come. Just like Daniel in The Lion's Den and The Three Hebrew boys, I know that I know, that he covers me.

God knows the end from the beginning. We have to keep our eyes on the promise, the future, the finish line, not on the turmoil or all of Satan's drama in between. Because although

Satan shuffles the cards, God orders the way it's dealt, this game, our lives are not in Satan's hand.

However, we have to be in that place where our minds and hearts are on God and not on us, because on us, Satan wins.

Satan is always on the prowl and when we decide to become lukewarm and push God to the side or out of our minds, then Satan gladly moves in, taking up tumultuous residency. Remember, Jesus came to earth, as a proven example to us, on how to run this Christian walk.

In Scripture, we see where Jesus so often stepped aside and sought that alone place that helps one to maintain focus. That place, where like Abraham, we will freely give up our best for him, just as he gave his best for us, no questions asked. He does not need or want our things. He wants our life, our whole heart, for keeps. He's concerned with eternity and he wants us as pure gold. He wants our heart fully committed to him. He wants us to get out of the way and allow him to move completely in. He wants total renovation. Smith's Wigglesworth talked about that place where he would not let more than ten minutes go by, without stepping aside to be with God. Intimacy, not some other men beliefs. While it is okay to listen to a sermon, how but being a sermon, like Elisha, Joshua, Gideon, David, and Paul, like Jesus. Hello! Aren't we supposed to be following him anyway, and not our fleshly desires?

Remember King Nebuchadnezzar was so big headed, he started walking around in his kingdom, the palace of Babylon, glorying in his accomplishments. Feeling like he was the man, just like me, he didn't recognize God at all. God did not just instantly, instantly, strip him of his kingdom; he stripped him of his mind. His heart became like a beast heart. His hairs grew out like eagle's feathers.

His nails like bears claws, he ate grass as an ox. For seven years, everything that he thought he had, he didn't even have sense enough to enjoy. He walked around like a wild, madman, unshaven and unkempt until he came to his senses and recognized, from whom all blessings flow, and belongs.

Never forget who the real king is, to whom dominion belongeth. The Bible says Nebuchadnezzar was an example so that all the living might know that the Most High ruleth in the kingdom of men and giveth it to whomsoever he will. (Daniel 4:17) In addition, just like Nebuchadnezzar, we must be stripped of carnality; we must get to that place of oneness; that place where it is all about Jesus. Remember, two kings cannot run one kingdom. Someone has to move the hell out.

Trust in God's love, faithfulness, and sovereignty. Step down! Lay down your crown and let him rule. He is much more knowledgeable than you are and there is nothing too hard for him to do. Let him rule in your world, your love, your life; and see if he will not make a difference.

And don't get alarmed or carried away with the shaking up. Whenever a kingdom is overthrown expect there to be some noise, some turbulence, there's got to be some uprooting to the other kings' specification. You don't have the same taste or the same style, so he has to refurnish to suit his liking. There is going be a change, welcome it.

Trust his breaking down. Know that if he is breaking and shaking, you can expect some rebuilding on a much more solid foundation.

Moreover, contrary to popular Christian belief if you are a child of God. God has everything to do with what happens in your life. God said it would rain on the just, as well as the unjust. He said in this world we will have many trials and tribulations, but he warned us to be of good courage for he has overcome the world.

Moreover, as the Bible states, every hair of our heads are numbered; not even a sparrow falls to the ground without the father, and we are worth much more than a sparrow. If God is so meticulous about our strands of hair that shed daily, how could he not have a hand in every other aspect of our being, our life? We give Satan too much credit. Even Satan knows who the real king is, why do we so often forget?

In addition, not every breaking in our lives is Satan. As a Christian God allows us to be purged and purified by whatever means necessary. He knows each of us right down to the marrow. He knows what we are clinging too, desiring more than him and he knows the necessary for each of us because he knows our adversary. He knows we are fighting a battle that we cannot win in our strength because the weapons of our warfare are not carnal. He is commander and chief of this army and we need to stay in tune with his voice to assure we are caring out his orders. As Christians, though we live on earth, we are citizens of heaven and like Jesus, we must allow the Holy Spirit to bear witness with us so that we can follow his leadings.

We need the Holy Spirit, even as Christ in the flesh, Jesus did not go out alone. Before Jesus started his ministry, he was led by the spirit into the desert to be tested, and he came out to do battle strong in the Spirit.

We do not like or understand the desert, but you see, the desert is where we gain our muscles. It is where our weakened flesh allows him to be Lord. We have to let him be lord. Remember we are made whole in and through him, not in ourselves. He is our strength, our strong tower, our hiding place, and all power belongeth unto him.

He wants to give us the desires of our hearts, but he wants us to first go after the desiring of his heart. His heart is for us. He wants the very best for us. Try him and see. He is not a man that he should lie. He is spirit and you can't touch spirit. He is neither the son of man that he should repent, as he said in the word, "Would he promise and not bring it to pass? "God would not only bless you, but he will bless you exceedingly, abundantly above all your little mind can think, dream or imagine. This world, man, everything belongs to him. He said in (Psalm 50:12) "If I was hungry I would not tell thee; for the world is mine and the fullness thereof." (Ps 24:1-2) "The earth is the Lord's, and the fullness thereof; the world, and they that dwell therein. 2) For he hath founded it upon the seas, and established it upon the floods."

He does not need our things, but we must serve him in love and in truth. He knows our hearts and minds and he wants all, not some of us. (Matt 10:37-39) In his sovereignty, God knew Abrahams clinging would be his son Isaac, so he tests his faith to the point of ultimate surrender, his heart's desire. Abraham passed the test and in the end, became the biological father of eight sons, including Isaac and thus the father of many nations.

God and Jacob wrestled all night. In the morning, Jacob woke up yielded, with a permanent limp and transformed from Jacob to Israel; now walking in the faith of his Fathers, Abraham and Isaac. states, Then the man said, "Your name will no longer be Jacob, but Israel because you have struggled with God and with men and have overcome." (Genesis 32:28 NIV). He was the ultimate con or trickster, but he recognized that no man can wrestle with God and win.

In Job, remember Satan went about, roaming back and forth seeking whom he may devour, looking to see whose guards were down. Jesus never let down his guard, he always found time to pray. Note, even thou Satan found Job's guard down he still had to go back and ask Gods permission before he could touch Gods property. Job was Gods property, a devout man of God, always praying for his family and offering up sacrifices to God on their behalf. Nevertheless, Satan saw Jobs fear, or what Job feared the most. How did Job end up in fear? God did not give us the spirit of fear but a spirit of peace, love, and a sound mind. You know if we give Satan even a peephole of an entrance into our hearts and minds, he will squeeze in and try to corrupt our being. If Job stayed in faith and kept his eyes on God trusting and knowing that even death has to respect the blood, Satan would have had to keep seeking and roaming. For there is only one king and Satan too must bow to him.

All knees must bow, and all tongues will confess that Jesus Christ is Lord. (What part of all do we not understand? Don't make the A and (a) separated from the double ll's) No matter what our belief is now, there is coming a day when he will get his due respect. God bows to no one, to nothing. He is and will always be King of kings and Lord of lords. God is sovereign forever, overall. Even the elements thou senseless are cognitive of this fact. For the winds, sea, fire, and rocks tremble, shake, erupt, split asunder and stand still in his presence and at his commands. With Peter all he had to say was peace be still and the waters obeyed, he spoke to the barren fig tree and it cease to bear fruit, ever again.

While in writing this I'm reminded of the story in Mark, where during the storm Jesus was in the back of the boat asleep; when the disciples awaken him, he rebuked the winds and waves by simply saying, "Quiet Down!" 39) "Then he rebuked the wind and said to the sea "Quiet down!" And the wind fell, and there was a great calm! 40) And he asked them,

"Why were you so fearful? Don't you even yet have confidence in me?" (Mark 4:39-40 The Living Bible) But though in his company day and night, I notice like so many of us today, they didn't have confidence in him, because though in his physical presence just about all the time, My God! They still did not recognize who he was, is and will be, for all eternity. We fear because we do not trust who the Bible says he is. Scripture says, "And they were filled with awe and said among themselves, **"Who is this man,** that even the winds and seas obey him?" (Mark 4:41 The Living Bible)

My God, this brings tears to my eyes, what will it take for us Christians, disciples, apostles, preachers, teachers of the gospel, the church, to take him at his word. To fully believe he is who he says he is and we can do what he says we can do. What will it take to start operating in the spirit, in his name? We read the stories of the Old Testament prophets and marvel at their experiences, but remember he said greater things than these ye shall do.

Moses had to believe, in order to part the Red Sea. Also, as I read (James 2:19-20) I have come to notice that it is not okay to just believe. For this scripture states 19) "Are there still some among you who hold that "only believing" is enough? Believing in one God? Well, remember that the demons believe this too, so strongly that they tremble in terror! 20) Fool! When will you ever learn that "believing" is useless without doing what God wants you to? Faith that does not result in good deeds is not real faith." (James 2:19-20 The Living Bible) Therefore we the Church, are not seeing or doing the greater than these, that was given, promised to us. Oh, Israelite children, where is the Joshua's and Caleb's of today?

In (John 1:8-12) it says, 8) "John himself was not the light; he was only a witness to identify it. 9) Later, it says, the one who is the true Light arrived to shine on everyone coming into the world. 10) But although he made the world, the world didn't recognize him when he came. 11) Even in his own land and among his own people, the Jews, he was not accepted." (John 1:8-12 The Living Bible)

Just like Nicodemus, we must be born again. Like the rich man, we must be willing to give up our little everything to follow him. Again, two kings cannot rule over one kingdom without conflict. Someone has to step down. God said you 'd find me when you seek me with your whole heart.

Are you ready? Really ready to pick up your cross, his cross? We are born sinners, into a sinful world, so you see, we have to get rid of that sinful nature. We have to allow self to break down in order to build him up. We are all fleshy, born flesh. Yet, God is a spirit, so he has to allow us to grow spiritually, in order for us to commune with him effectively. So that, we can know his ways, will, and heart.

How can you follow what you do not know? Do you trust what you do not know? In knowing his spirit, we can his guidance. So, we must get beyond us, beyond me. We must get into the spiritual, in order for us to effectively fellowship and be divinely led by the master. So that we can recognize his voice and assume his role in our lives.

After 911, the world took note and seemed to recognize that there must be a God somewhere, that there is only one king, but only for a short period of time. You know pride still goes before a fall. Just when the United States thought they had a handle on things, they forgot again that there is a Sovereign God up there. Nevertheless, our forgetting does not make it annulled, it just sends us to hell. No matter what we believe,

God will still be the judge of the world, sovereign, and master over all, not some, forever.

It's Still All or Nothing

He Is Close
To the Broken Hearted

To understand life and death, we must first see that the body and spirit are one here on earth, but they cannot reign together in heaven. For scripture states, "Flesh and blood (this body) will not inherit the kingdom of heaven."

The spirit is eternal, but while here on earth, our spirits need a frame, an earthen vessel, a house to dwell in, in order to feel, do, and operate.

To give a little more insight, I would like to share my first experience with life and death. A place I never taught I would be, however, in October of 1998, I found myself in a mother's worst nightmare. So many days driving home from the hospital I wondered why, how could this be happening to me? As if my kids and I were immune to sickness and loss, children with cancer were always someone else story miles and miles away or so it had seemed to me, until cancer hit home, hard.

My baby was now diagnosed with stage four neuroblastoma, a very aggressive form of childhood cancer. Moreover, the prognosis was grim. Nonetheless, I made up in my mind that with Jesus, in no way, by no means was cancer to have victory over our lives. Nevertheless, it did, because instead of acting in faith when all hell broke loose, I reacted in anger.

At one point, I had believed that my faith was as strong as steel, strong enough to raise the dead, but now instead of faith, bitterness ruled. The more I prayed the grimmer the circumstances seemed to get. Where are you God, I thought, why are you not answering?

Since I was a small child I thought I knew God, but here in this hand-tied, desolate place is where I realized, I only knew of him. I had no personal relationship. Furthermore, I could not understand where he was in all of this, or if he was for me at all.

Still, I thought I had faith. In fact, I initially even refused some of the more radical forms of treatments that the doctors were offering us because I felt that my daughter sickness was for God's glory. Even when the doctors said it was no more they could do, that she was dying, and referred me to hospice, I still felt that if God is God, death had no victory over her. I always believed that ultimately God has the last answer and the only answer that counts, and he still does.

Eighteen months after being diagnosed, she succumbed to this dreadful disease. And in what should have been a time of deep despair God taught me the true meaning of life and death. Where the spirit of the Lord is, there is truly liberty.

I still do not understand that overwhelming peace that enveloped and consumed me. All kinds of beautiful spiritual songs sprung up in my heart, in my spirit. Some I had not heard since I was a child in Sunday school. Rivers of living water was welling up and overflowing inside of me, songs so uplifting that amid death, I just had to sing.

In a time of death, I felt life and joy that just did not make sense, joy so strong; despair could not overpower it. Here is where I understood what David meant when he said, "The joy of the Lord is my strength." In the natural, I felt like I should be feeling brokenness, pain, pressure, and gloom but instead, there was peace.

This is when I understood what the scripture meant by "Peace that surpasses understanding." I now knew what it felt like to have Gods presence surround and envelop me. He promised he will be close to the brokenhearted and he is true to his word. In death is when I knew, that I knew, that I knew that God is, God loves, and God lives on. For in my time of bereavement, God did not send ministers but he himself came down, ministered to my spirit, and answered my whys. God ministered to me that death in this life, this existence is not death but life. God spoke to my spirit with such knowingness that Kristina had not died but that she was just beginning to live.

That this physical life is death, but Kristina was just ushered into the eternal presence of God, a life without end. Our true life, which is free from physical pain, tears, fears worries and cares. A life where the love is so real you can feel it in the atmosphere while giving me that spirit knowing assurance that what I was feeling was just a mere residue, a tidbit of his presence.

In his presence, there is no need to audibly say I love you because the love is just that tangible in the atmosphere. You feel it all around you. A life where the spirit sings songs that is so lovely, the earth can't even begin to match the melodies or lyrics. A place where the flowers and roses and sunshine and waterfalls and relationships blown fresh and lasting forever.

God ministered to my spirit that Kristina's present joy could never be camouflaged or counterfeited by any joy offered here on earth. To me this was not a still small voice speaking but a witness in my spirit, a knowingness beyond knowing, real, quickening, bearing witness with my spirit.

In addition, it made me feel envious and somewhat jealous and it gave me a new zeal for pressing on spiritually. That is why my spirit still sings. Mind you, I am no superwoman, there were allot of fleshy times, of feeling forsaken times, of feeling abandoned and alone times, especially a few days immediately after my baby passed. I recall sitting in my sisters' living room, looking out the window, over and across the parking lot at the street of cars coming and going and noticing that although my world had seemingly stopped, life just went on. I remember thinking, God if you truly loved me, why would you allow this to happen? You are supreme, all you had to do was say the word and she would have been instantly healed. I know, and I am still convinced beyond any doubt that Satan cannot even blow one strand of my hair out of place without Gods permitting. Therefore, in all of your sovereignty God, I wondered, why have you forsaken me? Why have you allowed this to happen?

In reply, God ministered to my spirit and said. I too have a child who suffered. He was bruised, beaten, mocked, spit on and eventually he too physically died. It hurt me to see him suffer, at one point in his suffering, he too felt as if I had forsaken him and he cried, "My God, My God, why have you forsaken me?" He too, for a moment wanted his cup of bitterness to pass.

He prayed and prayed. He was so heavy laden, burdened down carrying the weight of this world, that his sweat was like unto great drops of blood. As I looked upon him, it hurt me to watch him suffer but I stuck to the bigger plan and allowed him to suffer for a moment, so that you, Tina and so many others could live and fellowship with me in glory, eternally, just like I planned in Eden, forever. Kristina has fulfilled her purpose and although you cannot see the big picture now, you will understand later.

In addition, He said to my spirit, "If you check the Bible, you would see, that although people were healed, at some point they all eventually died. Contrary to popular belief, not everybody, no matter how strong his or her faith is, would be indefinitely healed; forever down here, because nobody was sent to earth to stay. Until the great white throne judgment, all must die." (Ecclesiastes 3:1-2) "There is a time to be born and a time to die, a season for everything under the sun," God said we will live forever, but not in this existence, not in this earthly life, this is not eternity, this is not it.

So, because your mother, father, sister, brother, child, friend, or spouse was not healed down here that does not mean that God does not love you. No one can ever convince me that God did not love Jesus with all his heart. He said this is my beloved son with whom I am well pleased. A Son who was without sin, but he came to live and die, God could have sent ten thousand angels and rescued him off that cross, in fact, he did not even need an army, for he is an army all by himself.

He could have stumped his feet and caused the worst earthquake ever, killing everyone who was against Jesus instantly. He could have instantly healed all of his bruises and scars, but he stuck to the bigger picture for our sins, for our iniquities, for our chastisement for us to have an eternal future.

He allowed, allowed him to be a sacrificial lamb, so do not allow yourself to get into a self-pity party or a God did not answer, so he does not love me party. Do not allow yourself to fall into any traps of the devil and for this short physical life, with all its pressures and pains, lose your eternal life.

Do not get caught up in thinking this here is forever. Always remember, we were only sent here to pass through and whatever pains, sorrows, and menial trials for a moment we are asked to go through, do not get caught up in thinking it is forever. Do not try to hold on to earth and give up Eden again.

Do not let Satan's wick devices trick you into thinking God owes you something because he gave us everything. He owns everything, our breath, our life, our loved ones, our homes. So again, please do not get caught up and give up Eden again for this earth, with all its thistles, thorns, and weeds. Trust God and allow him to minister to you.

Like Paul, keep your eyes always on the high prize and keep pressing towards the higher mark. Knowing that these present trials and sufferings are nothing compared to God's eternal peace and presence.

Everything is Gods, was Gods from the beginning. No matter what or whom he entrusted into our lives momentarily down here. No matter what he favored us to obtain, everything, all of it, is Gods loans. Know the difference between loans and gifts. Loans are for temporary use and are to be given back to the lender. Jesus Christ is God's Gift. Only the true gift is going to last forever.

No man, no money, nothing can take back the gift, or wash away the blood. So always keep your eyes on the prize, be wise in Gods eyes and stop head aching over the loans. Do not continue to elevate the loans above the gift. Be sober-minded, again maintain focus on the high prize, so that one day you to might be able to wake up in eternity and say, "O death where is thy sting? "O grave where is thy victory"

In my quest to gain a better understanding of life and death, God showed me that our life; is our being, our heart, our spirit, our breath. Our soul; represents our emotion our reasoning our logic. Our flesh, this body, blood, our physical being, dies. (Genesis 2:7) states "And the Lord God formed man out of the dust of the ground, and breathed into his nostrils the breath of life, and man became a living soul." (Second Corinthians 5:1-6) states, "For we know that if our earthly house of this tabernacle were dissolved, we have a building of God, and house not made with hands, eternal in the heavens." 2) For in this we groan, earnestly desiring to be clothed upon with our house, which is from heaven. 3) So be, that being clothed we shall not be found naked. 4)

For we that are in this tabernacle do groan, being burdened, not for that we would be unclothed, but clothed upon, that mortality (death, the corruptible) body, dust might be swallowed up in life. (The spirit) 6) Therefore we are always confident, knowing that whilst we are at home in the body, we are absent from the lord. 8) We are confident, I say, and willing rather to be absent from the body, and to be present with the lord."

First Corinthians 15:44-45, 47 & 50, states, "There is a natural body, and there is a spiritual body. 45) And so it is written, the first man Adam was made a living soul; the last Adam was made a quickening spirit. 47) The first man is of the earth, earthy, the second man is the lord from heaven. 50) Now this I say, brethren, that flesh and blood (our body) cannot inherit the kingdom of God; neither doth corruption inherit incorruption."

Take note that in the beginning, man had first a body. Life, breath, the spirit was breathed into his nostrils and he became a living soul; a thinking, functioning being. The soul of man is limited to the earthly senses, hearing, touching, smelling, reasoning, emotions.

The soul, emotions, earthly, dies. The body of man is this physical shell, this house, this corruptible frame that can be made deaf, dumb, blind, lame, paralyzed, and crippled; this clothing of life, this dust of the ground, dies. The spirit is beyond the senses, immortal, supernatural, incorruptible, and eternal. The spirit does not need to reason because we shall no longer just know in part.

The spirit never dies. It is the life, the heart of man. (lives). The soul-emotions, body- frame, and spirit-life make up our being. The most important part of our being is the part that never dies, the spirit; the breath, the heart of man. That is the part that God is most concerned about, that is why God searcheth the hearth of man.

While men look on the outside (the body, statute, frame, mind) in first Samuels it states. God looks on the heart, the part that will spend eternity in paradise with Jesus or in a lake of fire with Satan, eternity life without end. Immediately in death, in the absence of our breath from our bodies, our life, our spirit goes either to heaven or to hell.

God gave us evidence, reference to this in scripture when before dying he, Jesus lifted his head towards heaven and said to our Father in heaven, "Into thine hand I command my spirit".

Also, in this same scripture when he said to the thief on the cross next to him "This day, (not tomorrow or in the rapture, but this day) you will be with me in paradise." Meaning immediately upon his life leaving his earthly body. On the mount of transfiguration, although Moses and Elias bodies were dead, scripture states in (Matt 17:1-3), "And after six days Jesus taketh Peter, James, and John his brother and bringeth them up into an high mountain apart. 2) And was transfigured before them, and his face did shine as the sun, and his raiment was white as light. 3) And, behold there appeared unto them Moses and Elias talking with him" (the spirit never dies) so in spirit not in physical bodies.

However, in this earthly death, there is no second chance, either heaven or hell, we decide now. In scripture, the rich man wanted God to send someone to tell his family never to come to this place called hell, but Jesus told him, I went, I sent John and the prophets before me, whom will they listen too.

Yet he put this rich man plea in the bible as another witness, reference for us. (Luke 16:22) states, "And it came to pass, that the beggar died (Lazarus) and was carried by the angels into Abrahams bosom."

As Christians, we are Abrahams seed, the children of promise, just like Isaac we are a part of those stars that are too numerous to count. Moreover, when we saint, righteous in Christ shall die our spirits are taken to our Fathers' house until the judgment.

This scripture is evidence that the spirit of men never dies, although we are released from our functioning body. We still think, hear, see, and feel but we don't have to reason because we shall be known as we are known. Everything is naked, pure, and whole to the spirit. We now see through Gods eyes and behold, we are perfect, without a wrinkle, spot, or blemish.

Under the covering, through Jesus Christ, there is absolutely nothing to hide. Nothing to be ashamed of, that is why Adam and Eve had no need of clothing; there was nothing to cover up. For everything is perfect in Gods image. Spiritually we are no longer prisoners to a body that can be made blind, deaf, mutt or lame, for he is life.

Yet the being part of us is still alive, our real selves. Listen to this rich man. The rich man also died and was buried (the body) but listen to the living being, his spirit (Luke 16:23) lift up his eyes, where? In hell, immediately being in torments, (not singular, but plural) not past tense or future tense but present tense, before the great white throne judgment, this happened immediately upon death. And the spirit of the rich man seeth Abraham afar off, and Lazarus in his bosom and he the spirit cried out and said, father Abraham, have mercy on me, and send Lazarus, that he may dip the tip of his finger in water, and cool my tongue, for I am tormented in this flame. Abraham stated, "There's a great gulf between heaven and hell that one cannot pass from one to the other".

In physical death, we mourn a body in a coffin, but our real life is not over, in fact, it has really, only just begun. However, if you made the right choice you can say with confidence "Oh death where is thy sting or grave where is thy victory. For truly to be absent from the body is to be present with the Lord. All we have to do is just accept his sacrificial offering and live forever with him. For it is finished.

It's Still All or Nothing

Learn to Always
Walk by Gods' Spirit

A few days before my mother died in April of 2002, I remember riding home from work one morning, I worked the night shift. I hate the graveyard, but I would go now and then to put flowers on my daughter's grave and to make sure the area surrounding her grave was clean.

However, on this particular Saturday morning, I felt propelled to go to the graveyard. So I got off the expressway and started riding towards that direction, as I approached the graveyard that human reasoning part of me felt like riding straight pass, but that something inside, that unsettling nudge, I just had to turn in.

After entering the graveyard, I felt a strong urge to go to the right, but my baby was buried to the far left. I didn't know anyone buried on the right-hand side, so I couldn't understand this urge to visit that side. Moreover, as I passed a particular area on the right, I had a knowing deep down inside, with a settled peace that I would be visiting someone close to me in that area of the graveyard very soon.

In addition, an impression of my mother's face flashed in my spirit (mind). I didn't want to believe this vision, so in my mind, I said, "Oh no God, don't do this, please have mercy on me." I Didn't want to imagine a life without my mother, my confidant, my truly very best friend.

However, instead of sparing her life, God gave me a settled peace that lasted when I heard the news of her passing a few days later. A peace that persisted when my sisters and I were making funeral arrangements. A peace that stood fast throughout her funeral service, and settled when we stopped behind the hearse, in the exact spot I was being drawn to a few days earlier.

I was not able to go with my sisters to make arrangements at the graveyard, but I already knew where she would be laid to rest, God had taken me to visit that spot a week earlier.

God knows the breaking, hard places in our lives, and he will never leave us to walk in those places alone. Not when we belong to him, not when we are trusting and looking to him. A week before my baby died, in a dream I saw me and my two other children leading the procession, behind a hearse into Dade Memorial Park.

This dream was significant because when my baby died, I had no money, no insurance, absolutely nothing, not a penny towards her funeral arrangement. (I explained God's provision during this time in another chapter) However, shortly after her passing, me, my pastor, my sisters and my mother were riding around making funeral arrangements, and they were all leaning towards this graveyard in a whole other county; Forest Lawn, because it was the cheapest one available.

However, I remembered, what I so vividly saw in that dream about two weeks earlier and I knew that God was telling me to relax and leave the planning to him. I knew that she would not be buried at Forest Lawn. Because in my dream, I saw me and my two other kids, Kristen and Monet leading the procession of cars into Dade Memorial Park. And on the day of Kristina's service, like déjà vu, just as I had seen in my dream, me and my two other kids were following a hearse with a long procession of cars behind us, entering Dade Memorial Park.

As Christians, we have to know that there is more to walking with God. We have to know that God does not only listen, but he speaks to our spirit, to direct and keep us; to let us know he is with us. When you really put God first he will not allow anything, especially the big things, to just happen without letting you know; if you have trained your spirit to listen.

Is 30:21, states, "And thine ears shall hear a word behind thee, saying, this is the way, walk ye in it, when ye turn to the right hand, and when ye turn to the left."

Ps 32:8, says "I will instruct thee and teach thee in the way which thou shalt go; I will guide thee with mine eyes." If I must choose, I don't want anyone else but him standing watch for me because he never sleeps nor slumbers and he knows the heart and intent of men.

In (Is 45:2-3) he also said he would go before us making the crooked places straight. "I will break in pieces the gates of brass, and cut in sunder the bars of iron. 3) And I will give thee the treasures of darkness, and hidden riches of secret places, that thou mayest know that I, the Lord, which call thee by thy name, am the God of Israel."

If we as Christians continue to mind this corruptible (flesh) some of the kingdom blessings that were meant for us here on earth, as a child of God, we will not see. Again, flesh and blood will not inherit the kingdom of God. (Fleshy motives will not gain his blessings) The carnal cannot discern the things of the spirit.

To know God, we must know that he is spirit and that he speaks to us through his Holy Spirit within us, not according to flesh and blood or human logic and reasoning. Remember Jesus told Nicodemus "We must be baptized by water and by the Holy Spirit." (St John 3:5) As Christians, there is a deeper level in God that we can only get too, through the infilling of his Holy Spirit within us.

Remember scripture tells us (Second Corinth 5:17) Therefore if any man be in Christ, he is a new creature; old things are passed away; behold, all things are become new. (Eph. 3:16) Encourages us to be strengthened with might by his Spirit in the inner man.

The word of God is the sword of the spirit, it is part of our armor, God is the word and who can withstand God. Let him be your compass through life. It's our birthright, get rid of those bumper stickers that states, "God is my co-pilot" you have no business being in control. Get back under the covering, let him rule the world, let him be the pilot, he is a compass.

As Christians, so many of us stop or rest in just experiencing God as the Lamb of God that takes away the sins of the world. A gentle, quiet, do not invade my will God. However, the true richness comes from pressing in to experience him as the Lion of Judah, the Lord God Strong and Mighty, sovereign, breaking all chains, all yokes, bringing down strongholds; knowing him as King of kings. Get to know him in fullness. That is where we need to be as Christians, fully grown in him, not as passive little babies.

As Christ is whole, we must be whole and although we love easy, we cannot continue to survive on just milk. We have to build muscles and building muscles require lifting weight. Yes, there is coming a day when all babies must grow up and be weaned off milk and fed solid food. If we are to go out into all the world, we have to be strong enough to drink. You can't give babies wine.

We must grow up. We cannot be carried around forever. We were put here to lead as he led us, to impart as he imparted unto us. We were sent, commissioned, to go into all the world, proclaiming his glory, we cannot go as babies. We must be well fed, so we can stand with our backs erect and our heads held high. We can't afford to go out and be pushed down by the touch of a finger, or a sharp tongue.

We have to have muscles and strong backs. We have to be able to stand. We have to be sober-minded, even-tempered and spirit controlled, in addition to being self-controlled.

As Christians, we grow from glory to glory. I am still in this grooming process, I have not arrived, but just like Jesus, I will never give up on me. We have to stay in the fight until we are gold. Though you fall, brush yourself off and get back up. Never stop striving to be more like him.

We have to maintain focus and follow Jesus example, for he lived to show us that like him, we can live by the spirit why yet in this flesh. Jesus had twelve disciples who walked with him physically on earth, yet Paul who never met him in the flesh, through the spirit, contributed so much more to the church. Paul seemed to know more of him and taught more about him. Why was that? Seems like he had more of a hunger, he was a hundred percenter. Paul did not fear being out there alone proclaiming the gospel. While Peter and the others hid, Paul truly took God at his word and started going out into all the world, not fearing death, nor persecution. It seemed from the day Paul received his sight, he never looked back, but only ahead. In faith, he went not knowing, and not afraid, for the sake of the cross.

Paul was well learned and taught by the spirit. We only grow muscles when we stretch and exercise. We have to want it, in order to get it. Desire goes before conquering. Here are some more of the Holy Spirit teaching and bearing witness.

(First Corinthians 2:6-16) states 6) "Yet I do proclaim a message of wisdom to those who are spiritually mature. But it is not the wisdom that belongs to this world or to the powers that rule this world-powers that are losing their power. 7) The wisdom I proclaim is God's secret wisdom, which is hidden from human beings, but which he had already chosen for our glory even before the world was made. 8) None of the rulers of this world knew this wisdom. If they had known it, they would not have crucified the Lord of glory. 9) However, as the scriptures say, "What no one ever saw or heard, what no one ever thought could happen, is the very thing God prepared for those who love him." 10) But it was to us that God made known his secret by means of his Spirit. The Spirit searches everything, even the hidden depths of God's purposes. 11) It is only our own spirit within us that knows all about us; in the same way, only God's Spirit knows all about God. 12) We have not received this world's spirit; instead, we have received the Spirit sent by God, so that we may know all that God has given us. 13) So then, we do not speak in words taught by human wisdom, but in words taught by the Spirit, as we explain spiritual truths to those who have the spirit. 14) Whosoever does not have the Spirit cannot receive the gifts that come from God's Spirit. Such a person really does not understand them, and they seem to be nonsense because their value can be judged only on a spiritual basis. 15) Whoever has the Spirit, however, is able to judge the value of everything, but no one is able to judge him. 16) As the scripture says, "Who knows the mind of the Lord? Who is able to give him advice?" We, however, have the mind of Christ." (First Corinthians 2:6-16 GNT)

Before Jesus died, on Calvary he told the disciples that he was going away, but that he will send a comforter. He also told them to wait until the comforter (The Holy Spirit) comes. As

Christians we know, his Holy Spirit has and is within us because scriptures tell us so. (First John 4:15) States, "Whosoever shall confess that Jesus is the son of God, God dwelleth in him and he in God". (First John 4:13) "Hereby know we that we dwell in him, and he in us, because he hath given us his spirit. "

(First John 4:4) states, "Ye are of God little children, and have overcome them because greater is he that is in you, than he that is in the world." The Holy Spirit is within you as a born-again Christian.

(First Corinthians 3:16) tells us "Know ye not that ye are the temple of God, and that the spirit of God dwelleth in you? "In (Col 2:6, 7, 10 and 11) Paul advise us to walk in the spirit 6) "As ye have therefore received Christ Jesus the Lord, so walk ye in him; 7) Rooted and built up in him, and established in the faith, as ye have been taught, abounding therein with thanksgiving." (Meaning we have to pick up the sword of the spirit which is the word of God and build up his Holy Spirit within us.) 8) Beware lest any man spoil you through philosophy and vain deceit, after the tradition of men, after the rudiments of the world, and not after Christ. 9) For in him dwelleth all the fullness of the Godhead bodily. 10) And ye are complete in him which is the head of all principality and power". (Not in us) his holy spirit is our soul's longing, yearning, and completeness."

The Holy Spirit is our birthright as a child of God, so let's open the heart of our understanding, so that we will be in tune to the mysteries that God speaks in the spirit, for he said eyes have not seen nor has ear heard the things I have stored up for those that I love.

Note, "The natural man does not receive the things of the spirit of God, for they are foolishness to him, nor can he know them, for flesh and blood will not inherit the kingdom of God." Not just talking about dying and going to heaven, but the kingdom blessings he has for us here on earth as well, flesh and blood will not inherit it, because we take possession through the spirit.

We as Christians, have a responsibility to feed ourselves in the word so that we can pick up the sword of the spirit, which is the word of God. We can't pick up what we don't possess. Growth is not gained through osmosis, we must apply ourselves. We have to spend the necessary time with him, remember he is the word made flesh.

If we know his word, we know him. We must grow spiritually. If we continue to let our physical muscles outgrow the spiritual, our weakened, malnourished heavenly amour will not be able to withstand or be steadfast in the times of battle, and in the spiritual realm, the devil will continue to forfeit us of our birthright.

If we are not in tune; though God Holy Spirit dwells within us, if we quenched it, or smother it, when God presents a God opportunity, we will continually miss it.

In (Acts 13:2) The Holy Ghost told Barnabas and Paul to separate for the work he had called them to do. (Acts 8:29-39) Phillip was led by the Holy Spirit to the Eunuch to help him understand the scripture of salvation and to baptize him.

In (Acts 10:15-21) The spirit instructed Peter that he should go with the men that visited him to witness to Cornelius. In (Acts 27:10) The spirit warned Paul of the dangerous voyage while sailing to Rome.

In (Acts 23:11) while Paul was in jail the Spirit told Paul to be of good cheer, for as thou hast testified of me in Jerusalem, so must thou witness also in Rome. Although Paul was in prison, he knew what the outcome would be.

Later, in (Acts 28:30.31) it states, "And Paul dwelt two whole years in his own hired house, and received all that came in unto him, 31) Preaching the kingdom of God, and teaching those things which concern the Lord Jesus Christ, with all confidence, no man forbidding him."

(Ps 23:1-3) states, "The Lord is my Shepherd; I shall not want. 2) He maketh me to lie down in green pastures; he leadeth me besides the still waters. 3) He restoreth my soul; he leadeth me in the path of righteousness for his name's sake." Because I represent him because he is responsible for me when I seek ye first the Kingdom of Heaven and his righteousness.

(Ps 121:5-8) States, "The Lord is thy keeper; the Lord is thy shade upon thy right hand. 6) The sun shall not smite thee by day, nor the moon by night. 7) The Lord shall preserve thee from all evil; he shall preserve thy soul. 8) The Lord shall preserve thy going out and thy coming in from this time forth and forevermore."

(Ps 73:24) states, "Thou shalt guide me with thy counsel, and afterwards receive me to glory." I Love this scripture, meaning all of my life I am never alone. Until God calls me home, he will guide my comings and goings. (Isaiah 48:17) states "Thus saith the lord, thy Redeemer, the Holy One of Israel, I am the lord thy God which teacheth thee to profit, which leadeth thee by the way that thou shouldest go."

(Ps 16:5-8 & 11) States "The Lord is the portion of mine inheritance and of my cup, thou maintainess my lot 6) the lines are fallen unto me in pleasant places, yea, I have a goodly heritage. 7) I will bless the Lord, who has given me counsel, my reins also instructs me in the night (dreams) seasons. 8) I have set the Lord always before me, because he is at my right hand, I shall not be moved. 11) Thou wilt shew me the path of life, in thy presence is fullness of Joy, at thy right hand are pleasures forever more."

In (Second Kings 5:2-9) Remember when Elisha healed Namaam and Gehazi his servant decided to deceive Elisha and ran after Namaan telling him his master had sent him to ask of him a talent of silver and two changes of garments.

Note in verse 25) When Gehazi returned and appeared before Elisha, Elisha said to him, whence comest thou, Gehazi? And he lied saying, Thy servant went nowhere but Elisha said unto him my heart (spirit) went with thee when the man turned again from his chariot to meet thee. Is it time to receive money and silver and garments? In verse 27) He said to him the leprosy therefore, of Nathan shall cleave unto thee, and unto thy seed forever.

In (Acts 7:54 -55) when Stephen spoke of Jesus and the prophets the people were cut to the heart but he, being full of the Holy Ghost looked up steadfastly into heaven, and saw the glory of God, and Jesus standing on the right hand of God. (Seeing in the spirit) spiritual eyes.

I think one day when we get to heaven there will be many saints asking God, why didn't you answer this prayer or that prayer? You said it was your good pleasure to bless me? However, Jesus will reply, I did answer. I was that voice behind you that said turn to the right but being weak in spirit, your human understanding reasoned it out and you missed it.

One day when we get to heaven and God opens the windows of blessings that eyes have not seen, nor ear heard that he was waiting to release to us. We will be amazed at how being weak in spirit we so often missed it, because it didn't seem to make sense in the natural.

God is not a man that he shall lie. No, he keeps all his promises, but we must do our part and yes again, I am saying it, put on the whole armor of God. Spirit speaks to spirit. If we have smothered his voice, we will not recognize the mysteries he speaks to us in the spirit. Scripture states, "This I say then, walk in the Spirit, and ye shall not fulfill the lust of the flesh." (Gal 5:16- 17) For the flesh lusteth against the Spirit, and the Spirit against the flesh; and these are contrary the one to the other; so that ye cannot do the things that ye would." If we as Christians continue to mind this corruptible, (flesh) some of the kingdom blessings that were meant for us here on earth, as a Child of God we will not see. Again, flesh and blood will not inherit the kingdom of God. (Fleshy motives will not gain his blessings) The carnal cannot discern the things of the spirit.

Do not be like Esau, be thou strengthen in the inner man, so that you will not forfeit your birthright. Grow up in spirit and receive all that God has promised you. The blessings of Abraham, for we are children of the promise. Let his kingdom come, let his will be done, for it is the fathers' good pleasure to bless us. He does not want to withhold any good thing from us.

In (St John 3:12) Jesus told Nicodemus "If I have told you earthly things, and ye believe not, how shall ye believe if I tell you of heavenly things?" (Romans 7:6) states "That we should serve God in newness of spirit, not in our old nature." (Romans 8:1-9) "Tells us to walk not after the flesh but after the spirit for the carnal mind is enmity against God for it is not subject to the law of God neither can it be." (Romans

8:14-16) "For as many as are led by the spirit of God, they are the sons of God." 15) For ye have not received the spirit of bondage again to fear, but ye have received the spirit of adoption, whereby we cry, Abba, father. Note, 16) "The Spirit itself beareth witness with our spirit that we are children of God." Just so, the spirit beareth witness with our spirit of other things concerning God. We as Christians have to stay in tune.

There is another realm in this Christian walk and if we really knew the word and the power that God has made available to us from on high, we would seek daily to live in his presence, to dwell in that realm. For truly, where the spirit of the lord is, there is liberty. For through the Holy Spirit he revealeth things pass, present and future. He will take over our mouthpiece and minds. He will be our defense and our counselor.

In (St Luke 21:14-15) it states, "Settle it therefore in your hearts, not to meditate before what ye shall answer 15) for I will give you a mouth and wisdom, which all your adversaries shall not be able to gainsay or resist."(Note in Acts, he did this with Peter, Stephen, and John)

(Acts 4:5-13) "And it came to pass on the morrow, that the rulers, and elders, and scribes, 6) And Annas the high priest, and Caiaphas, and John, and Alexander, and as many as were of the kindred of the high priest, were gathered together at Jerusalem. 7) And when they had set them in the midst, they asked, "By what power, or by what name, have ye done this? 8) Then Peter, filled with the Holy Ghost, said unto them, ye rulers of the people, and elders of Israel, 9) If we this day be examined of the good deed done to the impotent man, by what means he is made whole. 10) Be it known unto you all, and to all the people of Israel, that by the name of Jesus

Christ of Nazareth whom ye crucified. Whom God raised from the dead, even by him doth this man stand here before you whole. 11) This is the stone which was set at nought of you builders, which is become the head of the corner. 12) Neither is there salvation in any other, for there is none other name under heaven given among men, whereby we must be saved. 13) Now when they saw the boldness of Peter and John, and perceived that they were unlearned and ignorant men, they marveled; and they took knowledge of them, that they had been with Jesus."

Acts 6:8-10, "And Stephen, full of faith and power, did great wonders and miracles among the people. 9)Then there arose certain of the synagogue, which is called the synagogue of the Liberitines, and Cyrenians, and Alexandrians, and of them of Cilicia and of Asia, disputing with Stephen. 10) And they were not able to resist the wisdom and the spirit by which he spake."

To know God, we must build up his spirit within us, so that we are in tune with his Holy Spirit within us. He said in (John 14:16-18) "And I will pray the father, and he shall give you another comforter, that he may abide with you forever; 17) Even the spirit of truth, whom the world (flesh, carnal) cannot receive, because it seethe him not, neither knoweth him, but ye know him, for he dwelleth with you, and shall be in you. 18) I will not leave you comfortless, I will come to you."

God filled us with his Holy Spirit to endow us with peace. He said the Holy Spirit will lead us, quicken us, and bear witness with our spirit of things concerning God. His Holy Spirit is in us to teach us, encourage, strengthen, and direct us. He said the Holy Spirit is the spirit of truth and he will lead us into all truth.

In (John 14:26) it states, "But the comforter, which is the Holy Ghost, whom the father will send in my name, he shall teach you all things and bring all things to your remembrance, whatsoever I have said unto you." (Through the word) The only way to know his character, his ways, is to know his word.

Therefore, we must feed our spirit in the word, worship, and prayer, just as we feed our natural body. When we are born again the Holy Spirit is a newborn baby within us. We must build him up, so that we are aware of his voice, in tune with his leading, so that we can know his character. Like Joshua, we must abide in the word, so that we will not be easily led astray.

Scripture tells us (Phil 2:5) "Let this mind be in you, which was also in Christ Jesus." But remember God is light and he will not dwell in darkness. Jesus once said in a parable "Who will pour new wine into old wineskins." God wants to direct and lead us just as he directed and led the disciples and prophets in the Bible, but we must sow to the spirit and not to the flesh.

We must recognize that God speaks mysteries in the spirit. He does not reveal himself to anybody. No, you must be the Spirit-filled body of Christ. He said draw near to me and I will draw near to you.

We must want this Spirit-filled, this intimate life with him, and not only want it but wholeheartedly pursue it.

(Luke 11:13) He promised in scripture that he will freely give the Holy Spirit to anyone that asks. (Romans 8:6, 8-9) tell us "To be carnally minded is death, but to be spiritually minded is life and peace. 8) So then, they that are in the flesh cannot please God. 9) But ye are not in the flesh, but in the spirit, if so be the spirit of God dwell in you. "

Luke 2:25-29, states "And behold, there was a man in Jerusalem, whose name was Simeon, and the same man was just and devout, waiting for the consolation of Israel, and the Holy Spirit was upon him 26) And it was revealed unto him by the Holy Ghost, that he shall not see death, before he had seen the lord's Christ. 27) And he came by the spirit into the temple and when the parents brought in the child Jesus, to do for him after the custom of the law. 28) Then took he him up, in his arms, and blessed God, and said 29) Lord, now lettest thou thy servant depart in peace according to thy word 30) for mine eyes have seen thy salvation. "

Note the Holy Spirit told him he would not die until he saw Jesus (The Christ) and the Holy Spirit led him into the temple when Mary and Joseph brought Jesus in so that he could see him.

In addition, note Jesus waited until the Holy Spirit as a dove descended upon him, and led him into the wilderness, to be tested by the devil. Moreover, he fought the devil with the sword of the spirit. (The word.)

Scripture states in (Luke 3:21-22) "Now when all the people were baptized, it came to pass that Jesus also being baptized, (remember Jesus told Nicodemus by water and the spirit." He won't tell us to do something he would not do himself, he fully leads by example) and praying, the heavens opened 22) And the Holy Ghost descended in a bodily shape like a dove upon him and a voice came from heaven, which said, thou art my beloved son, in thee I am well pleased."

Then in (Luke 4:1), it states, "And Jesus being full of the Holy Ghost returned from Jordan, and was led by the spirit (just like Simeon) into the wilderness to be tempted of the devil for forty days and nights."

Luke 4: 13-14, 18-19 & 21, "And when the devil had ended all the temptation, he departed from him for a season. 14) And Jesus returned in the power of the spirit into Galilee" (not in the flesh) see, even Jesus waited for the comforter, thou he himself is our comforter.

When he went into Nazareth and into the synagogue he opened the book of the prophets to the scriptures, which saith. 18) "The spirit of the Lord is upon me, because he hath anointed me to preach the gospel to the poor, he hath sent me to heal the brokenhearted, to preach deliverance to the captives, and recovering of sight to the blind, to set at liberty them that are bruised. 19) to preach the acceptable year of the Lord. In verse twenty-one, he told them as he closed the book of the prophets." 21) "This day is this scripture fulfilled in your ears. Jesus started his ministry after the infilling of the Holy Ghost."

Remember when his mother told him to do something at the wedding feast (regarding there being no more wine) he said my time has not yet come. Although that was his first miracle (the turning of water into wine), He knew to wait for the power from on high.

He said in (St John 5:30-32) "I can of mine own self do nothing, as I hear I judge, and my judgment is just. Because I seek not mine own will, (key) but the will of the father which hath sent me 31) If I bear witness of myself, my witness is not true. 32) There is another that beareth witness of me, and I know that the witness which he wittnesseth of me is true."

If even Jesus, whose all-powerful, knew the importance of impartation, who are we to go out fighting a heavenly battle with swords and wisdom of the flesh.

For as Christians he told us we are not of this world. We are a new creation in him and our battles (no matter how fleshy they seem), are not against flesh and blood but against spiritual forces in high places, rulers of the dark. Like Jesus, we must embrace the sword of the spirit, knowing, that it is not by power, nor by might but that we overcome by the spirit of the Lord within us.

Although Jesus had the twelve disciples, he never stopped seeking time away, alone to pray. Intimacy with the father is still paramount. Like Joshua, Gideon, Moses, and the Christians of old, who were tuned into God enough to know when to hold their peace and let the Lord fight their battles. we too have to stay in-tuned. We can't afford to let down our guards. Remember the scriptures stated that the devil left Jesus for a season. What about you? It's never over, not until we see him face to face. Remember this.

Note as soon as the Holy Ghost descended upon Jesus, Satan was there waiting in the balance to test and try to break him. Again, his sword was the word of God. What Satan meant to break him, strengthened and shaped him. For all of us, this wilderness time is necessary, it grows us up and makes us look up and within, instead of in the mirror. Because what we see in the mirror is not our strength.

As Christians, our spiritual strength comes from the Lord. It's funny how when we are going through the wilderness, we can't see the impurities being removed and the jewels being set in. All we feel is the hunger pains, the weariness, and the heat. The realities of the wilderness; but then one day when we encounter a person or situation that would have made us bark, and bite, we are amazed by the change in us. We can't even recall when it happened but now we notice that we simply walked away wagging our tails and that which use to set us on fire, does not even cause a spark. Now like an alligator, our covering is durable, not easily penetrated.

I can't even remember when I stopped cursing. I just notice that my every other word was no longer a curse word and I noticed that I was not as impatient.

You too will notice, that instead of questioning God about your difficult circumstances, in all things, you will begin to praise him. Simply because he is Lord, no matter what, just as he instructed us to do. You'll notice that your life is no longer all about things but so much more, all about him. Suddenly we realize that our eyes are no longer on us but now on him, moreover, we are okay. We start to see that old things in us have passed away, the comforter has come and now virtue is shining through.

John the Baptist did not even go out without the Holy Spirit, Scripture states, (Luke 1:15-16) "John will be great in the Lord's sight. He must not drink any wine or strong drink. From his very birth he will be filled with the Holy Spirit, 16) and he will bring back many of the people of Israel to the Lord their God." (Luke 1:15-16 GNT)

In addition, Jesus commanded the disciples that physically walked, talked, slept, and ate with him to wait for the power from on high, to wait for the comforter.

In Acts the first chapter, we see that the Disciples waited in the upper room until the day of Pentecost, when the Holy Spirit filled the room and descended upon them.

Note, (Acts 2:1-4) said, "And when the day of Pentecost was fully come (Why does he say fully come?) Because we are to walk by the spirit and not by our minds counsel. I don't think that we can walk part in flesh and a little bit in the spirit. We, as Christians has to be totally yielded and filled. We can't afford to allow human logic and reasoning to suspend u. We must know, that God is God and God alone and only him sits on the throne, not you, me, and we.

Again, it is not we that wear the crown but only thee. On the day of Pentecost, the disciples were in one accord in one place, 2) And suddenly there came a sound from heaven as of a rushing, mighty wind, and it filled all the house where they were sitting. 3) And there appeared unto them cloven tongues like as of fire, and it sat upon each of them, 4) and they were all filled with the Holy Ghost, and began to speak with other tongues, as the Spirit gave them utterance.

After the infilling of the Holy Ghost then the Disciples went out preaching the gospel and healing the sick. Just like Jesus, John, and the disciples. From the beginning of our lives to the end of our lives, the Holy Spirit is to be our guide and not we ourselves. Human reasoning and self-counseling lead to lies, deceit, death, and destruction. In Godly counseling, we find peace, prosperity, and life everlasting.

Note how King David's wisdom led him. (Second Samuels 12:1-12) read where God said to Nathan to go to David, Nathan told David the parable of the rich and poor man, and David became wroth hearing of the rich mans wickedness. Nathan then turned to David saying thou art the man David planned Uriah's murder in secret to cover up his infidelity, but nothing is hidden from the spirit. (Second Samuel 12:7-8) And Nathan said to David, thou art the man, Thus saith the Lord God of Israel, I anointed thee king over Israel, and I delivered thee out of the hand of Saul. 8) And I gave thee thy mater's house and thy masters wives into thy bosom and gave thee the house of Israel and of Judah; and if that had been too little, I would moreover have given unto thee such and such things.

However, David did evil in Gods sight. "Nathan told him thou hast killed Uriah the Hitite with the sword and has taken his wife. Now therefore the sword shall never leave thy house."

Yes, David was blessed but read about the judgment he brought on his household. His own kids just about became his enemy. Especially Absalom, who fought him for his kingdom while the breath was still in his nostrils.

His son Abnon had unnatural desires for his very own sister and after raping her, was killed by Absalom his brother. Absalom died by the sword. The baby David conceived with Uriah's wife also died, even though David fasted and prayed. To lose one child, is not an easy burden to bare. Because David brought the sword upon his house he ended up burying three of his children.

For every sin, there is a consequence and some weights, even the generations behind us, are left struggling to carry, to bear. Let this be our example to never seek self-counsel, for we are not warring against flesh and blood. A little err on our behalf can dam our whole household. Scriptures state, not by might nor by power but my spirit saith the Lord. Again, we conquer by his spirit, not in our own strength and reasoning.

In (John 6:63-64) Jesus said 63) "What gives life is God's Spirit; human power is of no use at all. The words that I have spoken to you bring God's life-giving Spirit. 64) Yet some of you do not believe." (John 6:63-64 GNT) Therefore, like

Jesus, who is to be our example, let us do nothing of our self but only that which the father saith. Let's stay under the covering.

He Knows the Real You

God knows just how to send you perfect peace, through every twist and turn that hell attempts to bring your way. I remember just before my mom and baby died. All three of us was lying in bed in my mom's bedroom. Tina had just been released from the hospital and my mom was exhausted, after just returning home from dialysis. The TV in her bedroom stayed on TBN, this night Brother Schambach was on, praying for healing. Me and my mom decided to join hands and agree for her and Tina's complete healing. My precious Tina, who was just three years old at this time started prancing up and down in the middle of the bed between us and screaming out, "Mommy! Jesus is me and your doctor, Jesus is our doctor mommy."

I can still see her, with that little peach outfit on. She had no hair because she was on chemotherapy, but she was happy with a broad smile, from cheek to cheek. Me and my mom both looked at each other surprised, while echoing each other at the same time saying, "Where did that come from?' We didn't even think that she understood our conversation.

Six months later Tina died. A few months later my mom said to me, "Nett, I now understand what Tina was saying. God's got a body set aside for me and for her that's not made with hands. Jesus is our doctor." About a six months later my mom died. A week before her passing, I went to visit her. She was in a deep, tranquil sleep. I woke her up and she stated in a startling way, "Oh my God, I was having the most beautiful, heavenly dream. It seemed so real. I didn't even feel like I was dreaming."

"I saw myself walking towards heavens pearly white gates. And in the distance, I saw this little person in all white, glowing, and peering out the gates, like she was anxiously awaiting someone. When Tina saw me coming towards the gates, in the distance and recognized it was me, she pushed the gates wide open and started running towards me with her arms wide open, screaming "Mommy, mommy, mommy I've been waiting for you. What took you so long?"

My mom said that she ran out of her shoes towards her. She said, "I was so happy to see her. It seemed so real, until you woke me up." She said, "You know another amazing thing Nett. I was in the kitchen the other day and I heard the most beautiful music. Music like I've never heard before, it didn't sound like anything here on earth." She said, "I opened the kitchen door and looked around trying to pinpoint where that angelic sound was coming from. It sounded like a heavenly choir. I can't explain it, but I know it wasn't any music from down here. That music brought me so much peace, it felt as if I was floating."

"Nett, I've been experiencing some strange happenings lately. I really don't think that I have long here. My mind is not even fixed on all this stuff anymore. All these serenely, satisfying, strange things have me longing for up there. I can now look around me at all these fancy homes, and luxury cars and they mean absolutely nothing to me. They're nothing, compared to this awe-inspiring peace and tender feelings that's been coming over me. I think God is trying to tell me to pack my things because he's coming for me, and this time I'm so ready."

About five years ago when I was unconscious in the hospital I remember seeing this man in all white, with blinding light encircling him, come into my room. I didn't have to ask, I knew instantly who he was. He stretched out his nail-scarred hand towards me and said, you've grown tired, if you're ready, I've come to take you home. And she said I said, Oh God, I can't go now, my kids need me. They all have so much going on in their lives. Let me stay a few more years to help them? My mom said that bright light started slowly dimming, until it vanished from the room.

She then said, although everybody still has things going on, especially Nica (referring to my younger sister.) I have to wash my hands. I'm truly tired now. This time, am ready to go. I was listening quietly, with tears flowing down my face like a river because I hate this type of conversation. I dismally said, can we please talk about something else, this is not the kind of conversation I came over here to entertain. My whole face down to my neck was now soaked with water as if someone had died. But my mom's face was glowing with gentle peace. My mom died less than a week later. I remember when I received that unanticipated phone call. I was shocked. I couldn't wrap my mind around hearing those words. Mommies dead!

I instantly grabbed my Bible which fell open to these words. "The gates of heaven have opened wide to welcome her in." Wow! wow! I thought, thank you God, thank you. Me, my sisters, our faithful pastor the Rev. Richard P. Dunn and some other family friends met up at the hospital. We stayed there until the funeral home picked her up. As we were walking across the streets towards the parking lot, one of my sisters pointed out this white van that was passing by, stating," That's the guys from the medical examiner's office that picked mommy up." We all instantly stopped in our tracks and slowly watched them drive off. **That was our one, our one and only mommy, that we would never see alive again.** I remember my sister Floramae reaching out her hands towards the van and screaming out "Oooh Mommy! Mommy" and then suddenly plummeting to the ground, momentarily passing out.

Later, we all gathered at my oldest sister Renee's house, of course, no one could sleep. Some of us sat on my grandmother's bed, the rest stretched out on her floor. We talked and cried all Night long. It was a blessing to have each other. It's a blessing to have sisters. Around 0500 I had a catnap and I had a dream that seemed so real, yet it made absolutely no sense. In this dream, my mom was running her fingers through her hair and she said to me, "Nett, tell them to leave my hair alone. I'm not worried about my hair or what people might think, tell them to just leave it alone." That dream seemed so real. I woke up and told everyone that I just had the craziest dream about mommy. I told them what she said to me in the dream and what she was doing, and I never thought anything else about it, until the morning of our family viewing. Theirs five of us siblings, all girls. Four of us instantly decided that my mom's hair looked awful and that we wanted something done about it, before anyone else was let in to view her body.

Immediately, there was loud cursing and a stirring up of uncalled-for confusion, stemming from my youngest sister. All the funeral home staff came running into the area. Me and my two older sisters decided that although it's four of us against one, whose set on having her way or making a scene, mommy would not have wanted this. So, my oldest sister kissed my uncle and told him that she will see him at the house, she said, "Cause I'm not doing this, not today." Then she motioned to my grandmother to join her. My other sister Mae and I was also getting ready to leave.

However, my twin sister Nease, who never relaxed in being bullied, decided that she was not going anywhere, and neither was she letting Nica have her way. She said, "I refuse to let my mom, who has always given up everything for everyone be looked on or buried with her hair like that. If you think! If you think, am gonna let you come in here, and run things today, it will be over my dead body!" They both reached out, over my mom to start passing licks at each other, almost tipping her casket over. My uncle Nung quickly jumped in between to separate them. Oh my God! I said aloud, this is what mommy saw, this is what she was telling me in that dream. Nease! Just leave it alone. Mommy said, tell them to leave my hair alone. Everybody in our family knows, that my youngest sister is a rebel without a cause.

This opened my eyes to the fact that the dead in body, is still aware of what's happening around them. My mom saw that this hair issue, would have destroyed her homegoing service, and if she didn't try to intervene from the grave that some of us would have ended up in jail, or even maybe headed to the grave as well.

In retrospect, that day, a week earlier, that had me brawling as if someone had died, now brought me so much peace, because I now recalled that gentle peace that enveloped mommy's whole being. And the glow on her face as she talked about it.

I know that she's in a better place. At my mom's homegoing service, my sisters were hollering and brawling, but I couldn't shed a tear. I kept on remembering what she said she felt. And saw, and I felt such overwhelming peace as well. I felt complete closure. God, do I love my mommy, my best friend and confident for life. My mom knew that my youngest sister is a rioter without a cause. Five of us, and one-person intent on tearing the whole funeral home down if she couldn't have her way. I remember my mom often saying, when turning the other cheek, and giving up her justified right. "Am chasing peace"

Can we even begin to fathom how big God is? He that created the eyes, ears, mouth, the heart of men, our very being, the founder, developer, creator of the universe, he that holds the blueprint of the four corners of the world. After all, the earth is just a resting place for his feet, this whole great big earth, is just his footstool. The wind is probably just his breath, him breathing down towards us. He is an awesome God, the rain just the mere flow of a tear from his eye.

The thunder just him opening his mouth and the lightening him placing a foot down to reposition himself. Ooh he is king. He is unfathomable, he rocks, he rules, he holds the hourglass of this world and all therein in his holy hands. He is Lord, and he still sits high and looks low and absolutely nothing in heaven or on earth is hidden from his presence.

Remember when Philip went off to look for Nathaniel and told him, (John 1:45-48) "We have found the Messiah! The very person Moses and the prophets told about! His name is Jesus, the son of Joseph from Nazareth!" 46) "Nazareth!" exclaimed Nathaniel, "Can anything good come from there?" "Just come and see for yourself," Philip declared. 47) As they approached, Jesus said, "Here comes an honest man a true son of Israel." 48) "How do you know what I am like?" Nathaniel demanded. And Jesus replied, "I could see you under the fig tree before Phillip found you." (John 1:45-48 The Living Bible)

In scripture when Saul was to be chosen as king, it states, 20) "So Samuel called the tribal leaders together before the Lord, and the tribe of Benjamin was chosen by sacred lot. 21) Then he brought each family of the tribe of Benjamin before the

Lord, and the family of the Matrites was chosen. and finally, the sacred lot selected Saul, the son of Kish. But when they looked for him, he had disappeared! 22) So, they asked the Lord, "Where is he? Is he here among us?" And the Lord replied, "He is hiding in the baggage." 23) So they found him and brought him out, and he stood head and shoulders above anyone else." ((First Samuel 10:20-23 The Living Bible)

When the king of Syria was warring against the Israelite king, on several occasions Elisha was able to warn the Israelite army away from the path of danger. In doing this, the Syrian king became very angry, thinking there was a traitor in his camp. He called his servants and asked who of them is for the king of Israel; and one of his servants said 12)" None of us, my lord the king," said one of his officers, "but Elisha, the prophet who is in Israel, tells the king of Israel the very words you speak in your bedroom." (Second Kings 6:12 NIV) Who revealed those words to Elisha?

In addition, when Andrew found Peter and told him we have found the Messiah! And brought Peter to meet Jesus. Even before Peter spoke a word, scriptures say, "And he brought Peter to meet Jesus. Jesus looked intently at Peter for a moment and then said, "You are Simon, John's son but you shall be called Peter, the rock!" ((John 1:42 The Living Bible) Yes, God is omnipresent; and all-knowing. Remember Cane and Abel, David, Uriah and Bathsheba, Ananias and Sapphire. There is nothing that can be hidden from his presence, nothing of which he is unknowing.

(Psalm 139:1-16) It Reads, "O Lord, thou hast searched me, and known me. 2) Thou knowest my downsitting and mine uprising thou understandest my thought afar off. 3) Thou compassest my path and my lying down, and art acquainted with all my ways. 4) For there is not a word in my tongue, but, lo O Lord thou knowest it altogether. 5) Thou hast beset me behind and before, and laid thine hand upon me. 6) Such knowledge is too wonderful for me; it is high I cannot attain unto it. 7) Whither shall I go from thy spirit? Or whither shall I flee from thy presence? 8) If I ascend up into heaven, thou art there: If I make my bed in hell, behold, thou art there. 9) If I take the wings of the morning and dwell in the uttermost parts of the sea; 10) Even there shall thy hand lead me, and thy right hand shall hold me. 11) If I say, surely the darkness shall cover me; even the night shall be light about me. 12) Yea, the darkness hideth not from thee; but the night shineth as the day; the darkness and the light are both alike to thee. 13) For thou hast possessed my reins; thou hast covered me in my mother's womb. 14) I will praise thee; for I am fearfully and wonderfully made; marvelous are thy works; and that my soul knoweth right well. 15) My substance was not hid from thee, when I was made in secret, and curiously wrought in the lowest parts of the earth. 16) Thine eyes did see my substance, yet being imperfect; and in the book, all my members were written, which in continuance were fashioned, when yet there was none of them." (Read Psalm 139 in its entirety)

When your mom and dad were being intimate, they did not know you were being formed or fashioned, but God knew. God knows your substance, every fiber of your being, your chemical makeup in its entirety, your every organ and tissue, how tall or short you would be, the color of your eyes, hair and skin, your frown and silly grin. He knew all your shortcomings, your totality, your being. While your parents were yet playing and fumbling with names, he already knew your name. Your parents had to wait nine months and then some, to get to know you.

Yet, while still a budding seed, God fully knew you. He sees all things even the heart and soul of man. Remember in scripture it says, "While men look at the outside God looks at the heart." (Psalm 14:2) says, "The Lord looked down from heaven upon the children of men, to see if there were any that did understand, and seek God." In (Proverbs 15:3), it states, "The eyes of the Lord are in every PLACE, beholding the evil and the good."

Yes, God still sees it all. Read back on Nebuchadnezzar, just like in the day of Noah and Lot and the Israelite children in the wilderness. He sees the violence, evilness, indifference, assaults, and starvations. He hears all of our complaints and just like Jesus, I believe, our all-seeing, ever-present God from whom all power, love, and compassion originate, sheds a tear when he looks down on what has become of mankind. Do not think for a minute that these tsunamis, tornadoes, earthquakes, floods, mudslides, and cyclones are perchance. No, they are not the final judgment, but they are judgments, warnings, nonetheless.

In our utmost disobedience, of these same-sex marriages, (in the beginning did not he create us male and female in order for us to multiply and replenish the earth). This taking of Christ out of Christmas, is not Christmas about his giving? Is Christmas no longer a reminder, of his ultimate sacrifice for all humanity. The taking of The Ten Commandments off the walls and steps of the courthouse.

My God, is not his laws to live by the foundation for all laws. If we all upheld, endorsed, supported his laws, there would be no need for a courthouse or a jail. We won't have to worry about thieves and murderers, liars, adulterers, idolaters or coveting of someone else's belongings, for we would respect our neighbors and their stuff; if we loved them as we love ourselves.

This earth is his masterpiece. Is not he still the founder of it and the creator of men. The bid to remove one nation under God out of the constitution. (please revisit the book of Judgment. First and Second Kings, and First and Second Chronicles; in the Bible) and see what happened to the kings and the kingdoms of those who chose to forget, who the real King is).

This Wade vs. Roe, pro-choice mess, as if the power of life and death is now in our hands. In his Ten Commandments, he gave us the choice. "Thou shalt not kill" Maybe if man did not commit fornication or adultery there would be no need to make that choice in the first place. He gave us a foundation. If we utilized that book, we won't need a plan B, for his plan A; Gods plan, is perfect in its entirety.

Yet, in all our ignorance, God just gives us a mere spanking, because of his grace and mercy, because he knows our frame. Because he knows that a man, born of a woman, days upon this earth is only short lived and numbered. He keeps in remembrance that we are but dust and fleeting. Fools die for the lack of knowledge but remember he died already so that we can live. In love just as a good mother cannot forget her child, Gods remembrance us and yet allows us time, to repent and turn our eyes towards home.

Do not think what is happening with our economy, is just a result of bad government. No! It's a result of poor spirituality. It's a result of forgetting God. This housing slum and rise in gas pricing, read the Old Testament, expressly the book of Judgments and see what has so often happened to those who forgot, that God rules in the kingdom of God and of men.

Remember, nothing happens without Gods permitting. Do not think he does not see, our all about me mess. I believe God often time's stands up and pause, remembering his covenant with men. That is why this earth is shaking and trembling and the waters erupting and breaking loose. The winds blowing out of control, picking up and tossing about everything in its' midst. Because they sense what we in our ignorance is too naïve to perceive, the breaking of our fathers' heart and his chastening.

I believe that due to his remembrance of his promise, the rainbow, after the flood, is why his whole fury, his wrath upon humankind has not poured out. Because of grace and mercy, we in our ignorance are not utterly, destroyed. Think on those hurricanes in Florida and Louisiana. Those anonymous mudslides and fires, developing and spreading all over California.

God sees the Sodom and Gomorrah lifestyles in these places. He sees the crime, the defiance the Mardi Gras in Key West and Louisiana the gay lifestyles in California. Yet the mudslides and blazing wildfires, the hurricanes, earthquakes, and tornadoes in diverse places are of non-effect. Don't let him really get angry, as with the Israelite children. There is absolutely no regard for God, just like Sodom and Gomorrah. Everyone is out of the closet, walking around proud and tall. If he did not release help for the sake of the remnant of these cities and states, if it were not for the few righteous in these places, it could have been another total wipe out. For some it was, some lost their physical bodies. Some never got a second chance to consider what truly last forever.

Even though allot of Sodom and Gomorrah's are being wiped out today, the world refuses to stand still and pay attention. Still, sin persist. There are people that refuse to take heed, to an all-powerful, forever present God, who will have no other god besides him. People are still pursuing things, when God laid out all these birth pains, to let us know to get our house in order, because he is on the way. **He is coming, Soon!!!!!** The story of Noah is a tender reminder, to not be caught with a lamp without oil. 911 sneaked in and that was not a big enough of an eye opener. Hell is still a one-way ticket.

Along with this breath of life that he loan, loan to us. Is not he still overseer of the earth and heaven. Foolish men that we are, though we might escape earths judgment, you will see. One day, the all-seeing, ever present, Judge of all judges, will bring all secret sins to court. A court where there is no need of a jury because he knows, he's seen it all. No matter how dark it was, he still had a front row seat, for he is light. Yes indeed, he was there. Remember he said, it is appointed unto men once to die and then the judgment. So, nobody escapes the penalty for their sins, except the dead and living in Christ, because he picked up their tab, he paid their debt.

Once more, there is a real supreme high court, where the book will really be thrown at you. There is a court, where the death penalty is certainly the death penalty because here on earth you still have a chance to be born again. So, take advantage of that death row sentence down here. That life in prison, this temporary life sentence. You still have favor, that's what that is. You still have a chance for repentance and thus eternal life. God forbid we escape charges down here and have to appear before the great Judge, after this earthy death. **Do not think that because you died it's over. No! It has only just begun. Because here is temporal, but there is eternal.**

Moreover, what did the Bible say it would profit a man to gain this whole world and self-gratification but lose his soul? Plain and simple **HELL**.

Therefore, while there is still a chance to be atoned, check yourself. Confess your sins. **By all means, let your case be**

tried and finished down here, in the low courts. Don't continue roaming around on Gods footstool and think that he doesn't see or that he doesn't know. For he is still an ever-present help in the time of trouble, whether it's trouble in your life or the trouble you brought into someone else's life; through robbery, idolatry, backbiting, murder, adultery, stealing, fornication, slander, gossiping or lying. Again! You might feel like it's clean, cut, safe, finished, that nobody knows, but God was there and it ain't over, yet.

Remember, the one thing we know for sure is that as surely as we are born, one day, one day, we will die. And after this death the judgment, and henceforth our final sentencing for all eternity.

It's Still All or Nothing

A Time for Everything Under the Sun

Time spent is like money used, once it's gone you never get it back. It's a very expensive commodity. One that no amount of money can buy. If you don't believe me, go dig some of those rich people up, out of their graves and asked them what happened? How come their funds couldn't purchase for them good health and eternal life., and let me know the reason why.

In 2012 I was working in the MICU in Miami. I intensely desired to transfer out of this unit. However, I was practicing being led by Gods' Holy Spirit, because I wanted a closer walk with Jesus. I noticed in scripture that Jesus said I do nothing of myself. He did what he was led to do by the spirit. So, although there were several openings in different areas of the hospital that I knew I would qualify to be transferred too, before I applied and stepped out I wanted to make sure that God had given me the green light.

My strongest desire was to move into management, but I only had an associate degree in nursing and management required at least a master's degree. I was in school to further my degree and education, but I had two and a half years left before I would obtain a degree and could apply for a management position. I put this matter before God, not about the management position because I was still operating under my own understanding, and under my understanding, I would not qualify. I prayed to God about what other positions and area of the hospital I should apply too.

Immediately I sensed six months wait in my spirit. I knew that sensing wasn't me and that it had to be the Holy Spirit because personally, I didn't want to wait not even one more second. I was disappointed in this word, which I knew was of the Holy Spirit, but I knew that no matter what, I wanted to stay within Gods' perfect will and never be in his permissive will. I was admittedly discouraged for about a week, but I stopped applying and searching for another position because I knew that I must wait. This was in January of 2013, as time passed I almost forgot about this waiting period.

However, one day as I was accompanying my husband in Boca Raton, FL as he completed estimates and quotes for his sprinkler business, my cell phone rang. I immediately noticed that it was from my job, thinking that they were calling to ask me to come in and work overtime I turned my phone down and allowed the call to go to voicemail. Me and my husband continued riding and talking, eventually, I decided to check my voice messages to see what they wanted on my day off. I listened to the message and instantly thought that I was hearing wrong, so I rewind the message and let my husband listen to it. It was a call from a Nurse Recruiter saying that they would like to interview me on Friday, this was Wednesday, for an Associate Nurse Manager Position. I said to my husband he said my name, but I never applied for a management position, because I only have an associate degree, do you think they called the wrong number? My husband said, "You never know, call back and see what he has to say."

I nervously redialed the number, the recruiter answered and surprisingly said, "Hello Mrs. Williams-Holt, thanks for calling back. I was going through my applicants an came across your application for a Case Manager, an application that I put in almost eight months earlier, before consulting God. He said I was looking at your application and I felt like you were more appropriately fit for an opening that I have as an Associate Nurse Manager. If it is okay with you, I would like to set you up to come in on Friday of this week for an interview. I had to work on Friday but there was no way that I would miss this interview. I worked in the interview time around my break time. In my spirit, I knew that all I had to do was show up and that position would be mines because I never applied for it. This was all Gods arrangement. I knew that God had set this whole thing up, when I checked the day of my prayer, I noticed that this date concluded my six months of waiting. My prayer was in mid- December and this was in mid-June.

As an Associate Nurse Manager, with only an Associate in nursing degree, while checking in Kronos for the nurses that worked under me missed punches and late in and out times. And while doing and preparing to do employee evaluations, I noticed that many of them had higher degrees them me. Some had Bachelors, Masters and two was almost finished with their doctorate degree.

I sat back in my chair and thought, wow! But God! Not by power nor by might but by my spirit saith the Lord. I was sitting in this chair, working in a management position for which I was not qualified through experience or degree, by men standard. But! Because promotion cometh not from the east or the west but by my spirit saith the Lord, this position with barely any effort on my part, came because I waited on Gods timing.

Ecclesiastes 3:1-15 (GNT) 3 "Everything that happens in this world happens at the time God chooses. 2 He sets the time for birth and the time for death, 'the` time for planting and the time for pulling up,
3 the time for killing and the time for healing,
the time for tearing down and the time for building.
4 He sets the time for sorrow and the time for joy,
the time for mourning and the time for dancing,
5 the time for making love and the time for not making love,
the time for kissing and the time for not kissing.
6 He sets the time for finding and the time for losing,
the time for saving and the time for throwing away,
7 the time for tearing and the time for mending,
the time for silence and the time for talk.
8 He sets the time for love and the time for hate,
the time for war and the time for peace. 9 What do we gain from all our work? 10 I know the heavy burdens that God has laid on

us. 11 He has set the right time for everything. He has given us a desire to know the future, but never gives us the satisfaction of fully understanding what he does. 12 So I realized that all we can do is be happy and do the best we can while we are still alive.

13 All of us should eat and drink and enjoy what we have worked for. It is God's gift." Ecclesiastes 3:1-15 (GNT)

I believe that no matter how hard we punch or kick or beg and plead if it's not our time, then we must stay in line and wait. Jesus told his very own mother Mary, it is not yet my time but since he is infinite and all powerful he had the sovereignty to do whatever he wants to do. So, he turned the water into wine.

John 2:1-11 (NLT) 2 "The next day there was a wedding celebration in the village of Cana in Galilee. Jesus' mother was there, 2 and Jesus and his disciples were also invited to the celebration. 3 The wine supply ran out during the festivities, so Jesus' mother told him, "They have no more wine." 4 "Dear woman, that's not our problem," **Jesus replied. "My time has not yet come."** 5 But his mother told the servants, "Do whatever he tells you." 6 Standing nearby were six stone water jars, used for Jewish ceremonial washing. Each could hold twenty to thirty gallons 7 Jesus told the servants, "Fill the jars with water." When the jars had been filled, 8 he said, "Now dip some out, and take it to the master of ceremonies." So, the servants followed his instructions. 9 When the master of ceremonies tasted the water that was now wine, not knowing where it had come from (though, of course, the servants knew), he called the bridegroom over. 10 "A host always serves the best wine first," he said. "Then, when everyone has had a lot to drink, he brings out the less expensive wine. But you have kept the best until now!" 11 This miraculous sign at Cana in Galilee was the first time Jesus revealed his glory. And his disciples believed in him." John 2:1-11 (NLT)

Also, Jesus told his own brothers it is not yet my time when they tried to urge him to go to Judea to preach. Judea where the Jewish Leaders were plotting to kill him. John 7:1-53 7 "After this, Jesus went to Galilee, going from village to village, for he wanted to stay out of Judea where the Jewish leaders were plotting his death. 2 But soon it was time for the Tabernacle Ceremonies, one of the annual Jewish holidays, 3 and Jesus' brothers urged him to go to Judea for the celebration. "Go where more people can see your miracles!" they scoffed. 4 "You can't be famous when you hide like this! If you're so great, prove it to the world!" 5 For even his brothers didn't believe in him. 6 **Jesus replied, "It is not the right time for me to go now**. But you can go anytime and it will make no difference, 7 for the world can't hate you; but it does hate me, because I accuse it of sin and evil. 8 You go on, and I'll come later **when it is the right time**." 9 So he remained in Galilee. 10 But after his brothers had left for the celebration, then he went too, though secretly, staying out of the public eye. 11 The Jewish leaders tried to find him at the celebration and kept asking if anyone had seen him. 12 There was a lot of discussion about him among the crowds. Some said, "He's a wonderful man," while others said, "No, he's duping the public." 13 But no one had the courage to speak out for him in public for fear of reprisals from the Jewish leaders.

14 Then, midway through the festival, Jesus went up to the Temple and preached openly. 15 The Jewish leaders were

surprised when they heard him. "How can he know so much when he's never been to our schools?" they asked. 16 So Jesus told them, "I'm not teaching you my own thoughts, but those of God who sent me. 17 If any of you really determines to do God's will, then you will certainly know whether my teaching is from God or is merely my own. 18 Anyone presenting his own ideas is looking for praise for himself, but anyone seeking to honor the one who sent him is a good and true person. 19 None of *you* obeys the laws of Moses! So why pick on *me* for breaking them? Why kill *me* for this?" 20 The crowd replied, "You're out of your mind! Who's trying to kill you?" 21-23 Jesus replied, "I worked on the Sabbath by healing a man, and you were surprised. But you work on the Sabbath, too, whenever you obey Moses' law of circumcision (however, this tradition of circumcision is older than the Mosaic law); for if the correct time for circumcising your children falls on the Sabbath, you go ahead and do it, as you should.

 So why should I be condemned for making a man completely well on the Sabbath? 24 Think this through and you will see that I am right." 25 Some of the people who lived there in Jerusalem said among themselves, "Isn't this the man they are trying to kill? 26 But here he is preaching in public, and they say nothing to him. Can it be that our leaders have learned, after all, that he really is the Messiah? 27 But how could he be? For we know where this man was born; when Christ comes, he will just appear, and no one will know where he comes from." 28 So Jesus, in a sermon in the Temple, called out, "Yes, you know me and where I was born and raised, but I am the representative of one you don't know, and he is Truth. 29 I know him because I was with him, and he sent me to you." 30 **Then the Jewish leaders sought to arrest him; but no hand was laid on him, for God's time had not yet come.**

31 Many among the crowds at the Temple believed on him. "After all," they said, "what miracles do you expect the Messiah to do that this man hasn't done?"32 When the Pharisees heard that the crowds were in this mood, they and the chief priests sent officers to arrest Jesus. 33 **But Jesus told them, "Not yet I am to be here a little longer. Then I shall return to the one who sent me. 34 You will search for me but not find me.** And you won't be able to come where I am!"

35 The Jewish leaders were puzzled by this statement. "Where is he planning to go?" they asked. "Maybe he is thinking of leaving the country and going as a missionary among the Jews in other lands, or maybe even to the Gentiles! 36 What does he mean about our looking for him and not being able to find him, and, 'You won't be able to come where I am?" 37 On the last day, the climax of the holidays, Jesus shouted to the crowds, "If anyone is thirsty, let him come to me and drink. 38 For the Scriptures declare that rivers of living water shall flow from the inmost being of anyone who believes in me." 39 (He was speaking of the Holy Spirit, who would be given to everyone believing in him; but the Spirit had not yet been given, because Jesus had not yet returned to his glory in heaven.)

40 When the crowds heard him say this, some of them declared, "This man surely is the prophet who will come just before the Messiah."41-42 Others said, "He *is* the Messiah." Still others, "But he *can't* be! Will the Messiah come from *Galilee?* For the Scriptures clearly state that the Messiah will be born of the royal line of David, in *Bethlehem,* the village

where David was born." 43 So the crowd was divided about him. **44 And some wanted him arrested, but no one touched him.**

45 The Temple police who had been sent to arrest him returned to the chief priests and Pharisees. "Why didn't you bring him in?" they demanded.46 "He says such wonderful things!" they mumbled. "We've never heard anything like it." 47 "So you also have been led astray?" the Pharisees mocked. 48 "Is there a single one of us Jewish rulers or Pharisees who believes he is the Messiah? 49 These stupid crowds do, yes; but what do they know about it? A curse upon them anyway!" 50 Then Nicodemus spoke up. (Remember him? He was the Jewish leader who came secretly to interview Jesus.) 51 "Is it legal to convict a man before he is even tried?" he asked. 52 They replied, "Are you a wretched Galilean too? Search the Scriptures and see for yourself—no prophets will come from Galilee!" 53 Then the meeting broke up and everybody went home." John 7:1-53 (TLB)

Lazarus sickness was not unto death and although Jesus could have healed him instantly, he waited two days before going to Judea because his resurrection would serve a much bigger purpose. There was an appointment time for his visit. Also with Jesus on Mount Calvary, when Judas came with the army to arrest and crucify him Peter in human knowledge and understanding thought that they needed to pull their swords and fight but Jesus knowing the truth, had to rebuke Peter, and let him know for this cause and time had I come into this world. This time of Jesus crucifixion was appointed so that he could bring forth the obtainability of salvation to all men. Like Ecclesiastes states, there is a time set to be born and a time to die no matter what we do. There is a divine purpose for everyone who lives for Christ and that purpose is not living forever on earth. It's living forever with Jesus in heaven.

John 11:1-16 The Death of Lazarus 11 "A man named Lazarus, who lived in Bethany, became sick. Bethany was the town where Mary and her sister Martha lived. (2 This Mary was the one who poured the perfume on the Lord's feet and wiped them with her hair; it was her brother Lazarus who was sick.) 3 The sisters sent Jesus a message: "Lord, your dear friend is sick." 14 When Jesus heard it, he said, "The final result of this sickness will not be the death of Lazarus; this has happened to bring glory to God, and it will be how the Son of God will receive glory." 5 Jesus loved Martha and her sister and Lazarus. 6 Yet when he received the news that Lazarus was sick, he stayed where he was for two more days. 7 Then he said to the disciples, "Let us go back to Judea." 8 "Teacher," the disciples answered, "just a short time ago the people there wanted to stone you; and are you planning to go back?" 9 Jesus said, "A day has twelve hours, doesn't it? So those who walk in broad daylight do not stumble, for they see the light of this world. 10 But if they walk during the night they stumble, because they have no light." 11 Jesus said this and then added, "Our friend Lazarus has fallen asleep, but I will go and wake him up." 12 The disciples answered, "If he is asleep, Lord, he will get well."

13 Jesus meant that Lazarus had died, but they thought he meant natural sleep. 14 So Jesus told them plainly, "Lazarus is dead, 15 but for your sake I am glad that I was not with him, so that you will believe. Let us go to him." 16 Thomas (called the Twin) said to his fellow disciples, "Let us all go along with the Teacher, so that we may die with him!" John 11:1-16 (GNT

John 18 The Arrest of Jesus, 18 "After Jesus had said this prayer, he left with his disciples and went across Kidron Brook. There was a garden in that place, and Jesus and his disciples went in. 2 Judas, the traitor, knew where it was, because many times Jesus had met there with his disciples. 3 So Judas went to the garden, taking with him a group of Roman soldiers, and some Temple guards sent by the chief priests and the Pharisees; they were armed and carried lanterns and torches. 4 Jesus knew everything that was going to happen to him, so he stepped forward and asked them, "Who is it you are looking for?" 5 "Jesus of Nazareth," they answered.

"I am he," he said. Judas, the traitor, was standing there with them. 6 When Jesus said to them, "I am he," they moved back and fell to the ground. 7 Again Jesus asked them, "Who is it you are looking for?" "Jesus of Nazareth," they said. 8 "I have already told you that I am he," Jesus said. "If, then, you are looking for me, let these others go." (9 He said this so that what he had said might come true: "Father, I have not lost even one of those you gave me.") 10 Simon Peter, who had a sword, drew it and struck the High Priest's slave, cutting off his right ear. The name of the slave was Malchus. 11 Jesus said to Peter, "Put your sword back in its place! Do you think that I will not drink the cup of suffering which my Father has given me?" John 18:1-11 (GNT

It's Still All or Nothing

Like Jesus
We are Soldiers unto The Grave

God our father, is a soldier, a warrior, we are to exemplify him. He is not a man that he should lie. His word the Bible tells us that we are soldiers. David was a soldier had to fight for years before he became king, although he was anointed.

Joseph was a soldier, had to be steadfast, immovable on bended knees, keeping his eyes on God. Although God gave him a dream he had to walk it out in faith for years as well. Daniel was a soldier had to endure the Lion's Den even as one of the Kings' personal advisors.

Many times, in the Bible, we read accounts of Christians who won victories and wars without lifting a finger because God said the battle was not theirs and it is not ours. God is in control.

I remember when I was eighteen years old and had just finished high school at Miami Jackson Sr. High. All my sisters had jobs at several banks throughout Miami, straight out of high school and it seemed I could not kick a door open, even with metal boots. Everywhere I turned, I heard a resounding no. After hearing the door slam so many times, I got tired of knocking. I started feeling helpless and hopeless.

Everywhere I went, wanted me to show proof of my authorization to work in the United States, which I could not produce because I did not have it.

I moved to Miami in 1978 when I was nine years old. My mom was paying this lawyer in South Miami for ten years to get me and my sisters Green Cards and every time we felt like this was it, that she was bringing us into her office to say everything is finished and we could go through the final steps for our Green Cards, we would find out instead, that there was another dilemma for which we had to pay more money. For over ten years we went back and forth, and we had absolutely nothing to show for it, except an empty pocket and bank account.

One day after being out all day from dusk till dawn and returning home empty-handed, I realized that my search was a lost cause. I realized, that I was not moving pass go unless I had the proper documents, because now the United States had passed a law that any company that hired an illegal immigrant would be charged a fine. And not only that, on the television they were showing Immigration Officers going on the job and removing people, just about every other day.

Anyhow, on this seemly God-forsaken day, I remembered lying down on my bed and looking up into the ceiling, trying to weigh my options. While asking God, what am I to do?

How do I get out of this trap God? Is there going to ever be, an opportunity out there just for me? Suddenly, I got a revelation, to get up early in the morning and go to the INS myself and fill out the forms for my work permit. This thought came out of nowhere, yet this was what I needed. However, I at once started fighting against it inwardly, because I did this before, about a year earlier when I was seventeen years old. I got up early one morning and went down to the INS office on seventy-ninth street and Biscayne Blvd in Miami. There I waited for hours and hours, when I finally I got to speak to someone to ask questions, I was told that I would need a sponsor who had enough money in their bank to show that they can care for me because the government did not want to bring any more foreigners into the country that were going to be a strain.

One bad apple could indeed ruin the whole bunch. Some lazy foreigners came into the country and instead of looking for opportunities, they looked to relax and grabbed onto every free government benefit they could get. Food stamps, welfare checks, and free government housing, bringing undo strain on the government. Of course, the United States was right, in seeking ways to eliminate this parasitic burden from continuing to happen. I asked how much money this person would have to have and what relationship would they have to bear with me. I was told that they would need to be a mother, father, or sibling eighteen or older or my spouse, with at least $10,000 in their bank account. My oldest sister was born a United States Citizen.

However, my mom had already asked her to sponsor us several times, with a flat out reply of no. So, I knew that this was not happening. For over a week I struggled with this thought that pressed deeper and deeper in and would not go away. I was eighteen years old and barely watched the news, I only caught glimpses of it when my mom was watching it. Suddenly something flashed across the screen that instantly caught my attention, God was confirming to me that this persistent thought was from him.

There was a new immigration law passed by the president, which allowed immigrants who were in the country for a certain period and was proven to be good law-abiding citizens the opportunity to get their work permits and eventually a Green Card. When I saw this, I sat up straight in bed with my ears beaming as if it was attached to microphones. Immediately after this broadcast I jumped up and started researching INS Agencies in other areas. I was not going back to seventy-ninth Street.

I found an INS Agency in Hialeah, on one hundred and third street. I noticed that people in different neighborhoods were receiving different and better options. I went into my mom's bedroom and asked her for my social security card, passport and for my Florida I.D card. I also asked her for any papers she might have had, from our stealing immigration lawyer. My mom asked why and when I told her my plans. Suddenly, she sat up straight in bed and became very defensive. You are going where? Just you without a lawyer? Yes, I said. I didn't have any money. Neither, did I know what to expect, but I was at the end of my rope and I had to either swim or continue drowning. I could not just stay here in the United States with my hands tied behind my back, trying to shuffle along. I could not waste my life. I had dreams of being and doing more. And if I could not move forward in the United States then, although I really did not want too, I would have to move back home, to the Bahamas.

My mom told me not to bring those people here, (to her house) or put her address down on those papers. She said, "When them people arrest you and deport you home, don't bring them back here to my house." "Everybody has jobs, just wait, we'll get a better lawyer. They're enforcing deportations now. You can't go down there by yourself."

I said I got to go. I cannot continue waking up in this stagnating, barren place. I saw on the news a little while ago that the president passed a bill permitting certain illegal immigrants to get their work permit and subsequently their permanent residency. She said, but those papers can be filled with trickery. You need someone with knowledge of the immigration system, to go over them thoroughly and, to fill them out for you.

I stood firm, and unbendable, for I was empty. I could not see it any other way but forward. My mom did not give me the papers, but I stayed up all night and ram sacked every box and package in her bedroom closet until I found what I needed.

That next morning, still half asleep at 0730 with only bus fare and about five extra dollars in my pocket, I called the local transit system to find out what bus I needed to take to the Hialeah INS office. Then as I was getting dressed, my mom heard me fumbling around in my room and got up to give me one more warning. Net, think about what you're doing, didn't you see on TV how they've been arresting people left and right, right off their jobs and deporting them back home. I only want what's best for you. You must do these things the right way, with a lawyer.

I didn't answer because truly deep down inside I didn't know what I was going to do or meet up with. I just knew I was going, because if there was even a caution light, that was a chance that I could drive slowly through and I needed to take all my chances. As I walked out the door, I said okay mommy, I'll see you later. She replied, "See who later? I meant it when I told you not to bring those people back to my house to deport my children."

I felt a little heavy hearted because that statement my mom made excluded me, or so it seemed from the family but me being as stubborn as a bull, that's what my mom and dad called me when I was ten years old. I remember my parents once telling me "You are not made of steel. You can either bend or break. This day, I wasn't trying to be hardheaded. I just needed to at least try something else. Something new. And I remember thinking, I was born to die, as I grind my teeth and took my whooping when I was ten years old. I remember making sure to refrain from giving my parents the satisfaction of seeing one drop of tear.

I didn't understand that statement back then, but now as I write this, I could see me in their words. I gave no reply to my mom, I just marched out and into the streets thinking, forward, forward. I had no thought for what might happen later or where I might be sleeping if I got to sleep that night. No, I was one hundred percent, every second of the way marching onward. I noticed every little thing around me. Every scent, every sight, every sound. I was one hundred percent in the now. I didn't know it then, but tomorrow like the Bible said would have to worry about itself.

When I got off the bus at one hundred and third street, I had to ask directions on how to get to the INS office. I met several people who gratefully pointed me in the right direction. And all though I arrived at the building early, I still seemed to be late because there were hundreds of people already waiting in line. There was also a lot of noise and directing from INS workers. I kept asking questions as I inched my way along through the line and God kept sending helpers every step of the way.

Although I was eighteen, I was always told that I looked a lot younger than my age. So, people kept asking me where were my parents as they instructed me along. This one Hispanic lady started outlining everything that I would need. I found that I had everything except a Passport Photo. She was in line behind me and she told me that there was a place that took Passport Photos downstairs in the mall lobby. I was told that the Pictures would cost between four to five dollars that meant I would have no money for even a soda, but at least I would have all that I needed to continue moving forward.

There were about two hundred people in front of us, she agreed to hold my place in line while I went to take my photos. Later, when I got back in line and came through the first line of questioning, and was give some forms to fill out, I ended up sitting next to this older Hispanic man who then told me that in this next step I would be asked a series of questions about the United States. And that I would need to know the continents and the colonies and the meaning of the stars and stripes.

He told me that I would need to know about the United States Congress the House of Representatives, the Senate, and the names of the former presidents, especially Abraham Lincoln and George Washington and that I would have to know the Pledge of Allegiance and the Declaration of Independence. He then shared the answers to some of the most frequently asked questions with me.

After waiting several more hours, I got through that step and went back to sitting and waiting. Along the way, the area got less and less congested because large numbers of people were being turned away each step of the way, for various reasons. Thank God, I was still in the race. After about four o clock I finally got my mini interview and left with a work permit and an appointment to come back in for an interview, for my temporary residency.

I reached home late that evening. My mom was in the living room, anxiously awaiting with a big grin on her face. I knew she spent all day praying. She put everything in Gods hand. I pulled out my work permit and then sat down and shared with her all that had happened. She told me that she prayed that God would go with me and that he would send angels to help me along the way.

God not only went with me, but he indeed sent helpers all along the way. Yes, the Judge of all judges will have the last say. I went back for an interview ninety days later and got my temporary residency. Eighteen months later I had my permanent residency and finally five years later, I was being sworn in for my U.S. citizenship, all without any help from a lawyer or money in the bank. I filled out every form by myself.

Later, I helped my sisters as well, who are also now U.S. Citizens, without a ten-thousand-dollar sponsor, without having to pay someone to marry them for papers and without dishing out thousands of dollars to lawyers. What we fought relentlessly, for ten years to obtain, God opened a door for us to walk through in days.

Can we even begin to fathom how big God is, he that created our eyes, ears, mouth the very heart of men; our very being. The founder, developer, creator of the universe, he that holds the blueprint of the four corners of the world in his mighty hands. This earth is just a resting place for his feet, this whole, great, big earth is just his footstool. The wind is just his breath; him merely breathing down towards us. He is an awesome God, the rain just the mere flow of a tear from his eyes. The thunder just him opening his mouth and the lightening him placing a foot down to reposition himself.

Yes, he is king. He is unfathomable; he rocks, he rules, he holds the hourglass of this world and all therein in his holy hands. He is Lord, and he still sits high and looks low and nothing or no one in heaven or earth is hidden from his presence.

Still, we are not to let down our guard, because this is spiritual warfare. However, there's a lot of ministers and televangelist preaching a pearly white, silver and gold gospel, sowing of seed for Gods favor. However, Gods love and kindness, his blessings are not for sale. His word says it rains on the just as well as the unjust. Therefore, we must never let down our guards; expecting all heaven on earth, because no matter what is down here, this is not it.

We the church, like Jesus are soldiers of the cross. That's why the Bible, scriptures, instructs us to put on the whole armor of God, to put on the helmet of salvation, the breastplate of righteousness and to pick up the sword of the spirit. That sounds like suiting up for a battle to me. Sounds like getting ready for war. The word, the Bible says, we are considered as sheep for the slaughter (to Satan) pressed on every side but it reminds us Jesus too was a soldier pressed and persecuted, had to endure the cross, so that we may live.

The truth is, God is true to all his words. The word tells us to count it all joy, everything, he never said it would be easy. In fact, he said in (John 15:18-24) "If the world hates you, ye know that it hated me before it hated you. 19) If ye were of the world, the world would love his own: but I have chosen you out of the world, therefore the world hateth you. 20) Remember the word that I said unto you, the servant is not greater than his Lord. If they have persecuted me, they will also persecute you; if they have kept my saying, they will keep yours also. 21) But all these things will they do unto you for my name's sake, because they know not him that sent me. 22) Listen to this, "If I had not come and spoken unto them, they had not sin; but now they have no cloke for their sin." (now they know the truth) 25) But this cometh to pass, that the word, might be fulfilled that is written in their law, they hated me without a cause."

(Second Tim 2:3-4&11-12)"Thou therefore endure hardness, as a good soldier of Jesus Christ. 4) No man that warreth entangleth himself with the affairs of this life; that he may please him who hath chosen him to be a soldier. 11) It is a faithful saying: For if we be dead with him, we shall also live with him: 12) If we suffer, we shall also reign with him; if we deny him, he also will deny us."

However, Jesus gave us a mark to focus on and he did not leave us comfortless. He left the Holy Ghost. He told us he has overcome the world; hardship, temptations, and persecutions. He told the rich man to follow him not wealth. We too must follow his example, like Nicodemus we must be born again, not of flesh but in spirit, because God is a spirit. (John 4:24) Though we are born flesh, remember scripture states, "Flesh and blood will not inherit the kingdom of God"

(First Corinthians 15:50) In addition, our weapons of warfare are not carnal (second Corinthians 10:4) they are spiritual. Therefore, we cannot win in the natural, with ordinary human wisdom and strength. When we are born again, our flesh is going to have to die, for us to be whole, in Christ. We must reflect our father in spirit and in truth.

We have to take on Gods' nature, we can't go on being adulterers, whoremongers, liars, backbiters, killing, stealing, gossiping and being idolaters, men loving men and women loving women. These are reflections of the adversary; the devil, these are his characteristics. He is deceitful and selfish, and a lover only of himself.

Christ in his unselfish nature so loved the world, that he gave his life for us. So, no, we cannot go on representing Satan while identifying ourselves with God's name. (Christian) We have to starve the hell out of this flesh, pick up the sword of the spirit and grow. We have to become a new creation in Christ. Because while God is concerned about our having material things, he is so much more concerned about our souls, our maturity in spirit, in him. That is where our strength lies.

Remember we were sent to be a light, to be the salt of the earth, to add flavor, seasoning to it, not to blend in.

Therefore, God is not going to allow us to go around blowing out other people's candle, his beam in them, by our resemblance of a hypocrite to them. We are to disciple and strengthen in Christ, not in earthly wealth.

I know Christians do not want to hear this, but did not scriptures say, "For whom the Lord loveth he chasteneth, and scourgeth every son whom he receiveth." (Hebrew 12:6) Our kids reflect us and represent us, even when they're not in our presence because they carry our name. We as parents are supposed to instill Godly wisdom, values, and principles in our kids. But lately, in this world of babies (teenagers) having and raising baby's morals and values, pride, and dignity, integrity has taken a back seat. However, God is not taking a back seat. We are going to reflect him.

We are going to put on a new nature. Old things of Satan are going to have to pass away (If you want to truly walk in the fullness of the faith) in our lives because sin is not going to continue to reign. Sin is not going to enter heaven. Those Ten Commandments are not just suggestions. They are not negotiable to us who call ourselves Christians, but that's how so many of our churches are treating them. That is why we are losing our children. Remember they are Gods laws to live by. Laws he commands us to do, commandments. God is faithful and just to forgive our sins, but we are not going to be playing born again.

Remember Saul, Ananias, and Sapphira, Elias sons, even Samuel, although he was a prophet his sons were not worthy to rule in his stead as a priest. God will not be mocked, God is divinity and love, but love must be tough, or we will all succumb to this earthen vessel, and end up in hell.

Remember what was said in (Revelation 3:15-22, "I know you well you are neither hot nor cold; I wish you were one or the other! 16) But since you are merely lukewarm, I will spit you out of my mouth! 17) "You say, 'I am rich, with everything I want; I don't need a thing!' And you don't realize that spiritually you are wretched and miserable and poor and blind and naked. 18) "My advice to you is to buy pure gold from me, gold purified by fire-only then will you truly be rich. And to purchase from me white garments, clean and pure, so you won't be naked and ashamed; and to get medicine from me to heal your eyes and give you back your sight. 19) I continually discipline and punish everyone I love; so I must punish you, unless you turn from your indifference and become enthusiastic about the things of God. 20) "Look! I have been standing at the door and I am constantly knocking. If anyone hears me calling him and opens the door, I will come in and fellowship with him and he with me. 21) I will let everyone who conquers sit beside me on my throne, just as I took my place with my Father on his throne when I had conquered. 22) Let those who can hear, listen to what the Spirit is saying to the churches." (Revelation 3:15-22, The Living Bible)

Note, not to the world but what the spirit is saying to the churches. We can't be in church on Sunday and in the world the rest of the week and think that God does not care or see. We can't serve two masters. We the church have to wake up today. Moreover, check ourselves. Why are we losing a battle that he has already won? Like the Israelite children, why are we walking around in the desert? When there is sickness, death, divorce, famine, nakedness, homelessness, sin just running rampant in our midst. Why are we not conquering?

I say we must, must choose this day whom we will serve. We must get serious about God, just as he was serious about us, in laying down his life. As children, we have to be and will be corrected and redirected until we get it right. Scripture says, "He that spareth his rod hateth his son: but he that loveth him chasteneth him betimes." (Early) (Proverbs 13:24). God is love; do you think he is going to spare his rod for you? Do you think he is going to just sit back and allow you to go to hell? No matter what we do in secret our all-seeing, all knowing, all loving, faithful father is not going to sit back and let us cater to these jars of clay and end up in hell.

Tough love is going to fight for you until you are steadfast, immovable, and remade anew. Until you know whose and whom you are in Christ. Until no counterfeit pleasures can sway your eyes or heart. Tough love is going to keep reaching down and pulling you up, but your baggage is going to be pushed off as you elevate, so that you will never again have to endure its weight. (This is when you truly decide to get serious about God) Tough love is going to beam on you until you are a light shining bright like he is. Until he can see his reflection in you, until he can look down on you and say with pride, that is my child, yeah that one is with me.

As Christian, like our father, we are primarily soldiers of the cross and remember this is a fight unto death. So again, do not lose focus and put down your guard, because if you give Satan even a peephole of an entrance he will squeeze his way in and blow your whole house down. Always remember scripture says, "To put on the whole armor of God that ye may be able to stand against the wiles (trickery, maneuvers, cunning) of the devil." (Ephesians 6:11), note, not just part of his amour; because these earthen vessels, these jars of clay we live in on earth is vulnerable to the pressures of this world, they are easily penetrated by all that we live around. We cannot live in the world and not be affected by the world.

Moreover, to stand fast in Christ despite whatever happens. We need the breastplate of righteousness to cover our heart. We have to pick up and plant the sword of the spirit deep within us, so that we are rooted and grounded in the word, not in the world. We have to put on the helmet of salvation to keep our minds sober, even-tempered, and controlled in turmoil and troubled times. So, we can hear what the spirit is saying. What thus saith the lord.

We have to keep things in the proper perspective, in the spirit, like Jesus. If you note as a son, Jesus always found time alone to pray and to be alone with God. Like he instructed (Joshua 1:8) saying "This book of the law shall not depart out of thy mouth; but thou shalt meditate therein day and night, that thou mayest observe to do according to all that is written therein; for then thou shalt make thy way prosperous and then thou shalt have good success." If you want to be successful here is the key, in the map of life, his word.

Do you truly want to experience the fullness and the goodness of God? Do you want your way to be prosperous? Remember we war not against flesh and blood. Our warfare is spiritual forces we cannot see with the natural eyes. Therefore, we surely can't defeat them with natural strength. No, we have to take on the Holy Spirit and count it all lost, everything. We must keep our hearts and minds, our eyes on the high prize. On who is ahead of us, Jesus Christ our big brother and not on what is around us.

Jesus is to be our example of righteousness. Jesus is to be our everything, our aim, our goal, our dream. I never recall seeing in scripture an address; a residence where he lived, a boat he owned or a camel he owned. While we're looking and expecting a life of glitter and gleam, I recall his ministry being one of unjust persecution and pain. He was wealthy but not in material things. Nor do I recall these things being his aim. Jesus walked on feet, Jesus was an evangelist, going from city to city just like he instructs us to go, into all the world baptizing men in the name of the father, the son, and the Holy Ghost. That is what he did.

In (Matthew 11:4-5) When John asked art thou he that should come? "Jesus answered and said unto them, Go and shew John again those things which ye do hear and see: 5) The blind receive their sight, and the lame walk, the lepers are cleansed, and the deaf hears, the dead are raised up, and the poor have the gospel preached to them." Jesus came and took back what the devil had stolen; he is the restorer of the breach.

In (St. Matthew 10:5-10) Jesus commanded the disciples saying go not into the way of the Gentiles, and into any city of the Samaritans enter ye not; But go rather to the lost sheep of the house of Israel. 7) And as ye go, preach, saying, The Kingdom of heaven is at hand. 8) Heal the sick, cleanse the lepers, and raise the dead, cast out devils: freely (freely) ye have received, freely give. 9) Provide neither gold, nor silver, nor brass in your purse, 10) nor scrip for your journey, neither two coats, neither shoes, nor yet staves: "for the workman is worthy of his meat. (Matthew 10:39) states, "He that findeth his life shall lose it; and he that loseth his life for my sake shall find it."

As Christians we are supposed to follow Christ example, he is the son in whom our father is well pleased. We are supposed to be doing the things that Jesus did. For he said these signs shall follow who? Those that believe. (St Mark 16:15-18) States "And he said unto them, go ye into all the world, and preach the gospel to every creature. 16) He that believeth and is baptized shall be saved; but he that believeth not shall be damned. 17) And these signs shall follow them that believe; "In my name shall they cast out devils; they shall speak with new tongues; 18) They shall take up serpents; and if they drink any deadly thing, it shall not hurt them; they shall lay hands on the sick, and they shall recover." That is why Jesus came into the world, to set the captive free, to proclaim the good news of the gospel, to heal the sick.

Jesus raised the dead, opened blind eyes and he did not always meet with favoritism. A few times, he had to escape vicious, evil men whose intent was to kill him. However, it was not yet his time. While men were fishing for fish to make money, Jesus was fishing for souls.

Again, knowing that he was now in a fleshy body Jesus always went away alone to spend time with the father in pray. Jesus found time away from the disciples and people to strengthen himself spiritually and we must make time also to strengthen ourselves in spirit, this is paramount.

Remember even Paul said I did not confer with flesh and blood. He conferred with the Father, he conferred with the Holy Spirit. Remember, Paul, Peter and the disciples preached Jesus Christ and him crucified. Their focus was not earthly prosperity, they never loss focus of Jesus birth, life, death, and resurrection. They fed the poor and supported each other financially in ministry. Theirs was not a me get rich gospel, while my fellow Christian brothers and sisters go hungry, naked, and homeless.

We are one; it's about us the body of Christ. There is strength in unity, not in just me. What is happening with the church today? We cannot carry these things to heaven with us. We can only carry souls. We must keep that as our aim, while things are okay to have, we cannot continue to allow things to have us.

Never forget the cross. He died, gave it all up so that we may live. We cannot afford to become complacent, hell was not made for humans and we cannot take back a dead soul that is eternally lost. Only the now living can still claim his cross.

Moreover, we Christians are going to be held accountable for losing focus. Like Peter and Paul, we are supposed to be disciples, apostles fighting for souls. We are his bride, his helpmate. We have to remember whose team we are on. We cannot let Satan blind us with temporal things. When our bridegroom (who is Christ Jesus) cometh he should see and find that we are still one.

That his father is our father, that we truly share his dream, that like him we did not lie down the cross, but maintained his focus, his purpose the loss. We should have the same heartbeat as him, the same mind, and the same goal, for we are one. Remember, no matter what the world has to offer, it will one day be a was, but God always and forever is.

Do not forget Calvary, his cross, his blood, his wounds, his death, his life, his resurrection. It wasn't easy. Remember him praying in agony, his sweat was likening unto great drops of blood, just bearing the anticipation, of the weight, of the sins of this world. (Luke 22:44) Sins that was in his time, that are now and that are still to come, over two thousand years of sinning. Please do not make Calvary of non-effect.

Do not make easy your goal. Do not make wealth your goal. (read the word) Jesus never said it would be easy, like Jesus, keep focused on souls, on being his sons and daughters, on being his bride, on his death, on his goal. Do not forget Gethsemane, do not forget Mount Calvary. Follow the mark of Christ and Christ alone, earth wholes for us no lasting throne.

Not saying there's anything wrong with things, just saying when we live in a world where our kids are going to school in the morning for an education and being removed in body bags, we need to see that we the church have let down our guards. We must regain focus. We must get back to preaching

Jesus, to preaching life, to giving hope, to exemplifying unconditional love.

For things will never satisfy or fill His space. Nothing on earth can take his place. (In us) Remember Paul told us to keep our eyes on the high prize, to keep our minds on what is true, on things eternal. Let's take our streets back, our schools back. My God must I say it, let's take our churches back, for the sake of the cross. Let's get back into our rightful places, let's get back to Pentecost.

We cannot continue being an adulterous wife to him and expect to see a change. Remember it is not about us; it is still all about him. He is king, he rules. He died to impart his spirit, all we have to do is accept him and let him rule in our lives. For scripture states" It is not by might nor by power but my by spirit saith the Lord" (Zech 4:6) I think I will keep re-emphasizing this scripture. In the flesh we cannot conquer or bring down spiritual strongholds, we can't fight Satan with flesh and blood.

However, we in Christ are more than conquerors. His Holy Spirit strengthens us. So, rise up and get back in the fight, ye soldiers of the cross, ye sons and daughters of the true and living God, for he is alive in and through us on the earth. Let our bodies be readily available to him.

It's Still All or Nothing

It's Still All or Nothing

Faith Is What You Do

My mother was the prime example of faith. I remember when we moved over here from the Bahamas, where to me, we seemed to have everything. In the Bahamas, we had a house about two blocks from the bay. We had a large front and backyard and plenty of fruit and vegetable trees.

There we could quickly go and pick bananas, sugar canes, supper dillies, guavas, avocados, sugar plums, papayas, sea grapes, and coconuts. We had a swing set with the sliding boards, and the sea saw attached. We had our favorite cousin named Lil Eric, who was more like a brother. He was always with us. And we had a pet dog named Father Joseph, who slept where ever we slept and followed us wherever we went.

Father Joseph would walk us to school every morning and seem to know what time we would be in physical education. Because he would be there, alongside the fence wiggling his tail without skipping a beat, every day. As soon as the school bell rung at the end of each school day we would find him running back and forth around the school gate, like a mad dog, enthused with the anticipation of us finally coming home.

Father Joseph was more than a pet, he was our best friend. He would follow us anywhere, rain or sunshine. And if anyone appeared to be harming any of us he would not hesitate to run to our defense. In the Bahamas where we lived, we didn't have any nearby parks, but we had a beautiful bay where the kids would gather on weekends and after school, to go swimming.

On one of these occasions, our neighbor Clammy frolicking around accidentally pushed my oldest sister into the deeper rocky part of the bay water. My sister was about eleven years old; my cousin Lil Eric and Father Joseph immediately jumped in to save her. While the rest of us kids, about eight or nine of us stood by watching anxiously and screaming.

We just knew that they would surely die, because the waters were raging and roaring furiously, and the waves on this particular day seemed almost ten feet tall. It was definitely not swimming water, hammering against the bank of the bay.

My sister went down and after what seems like forever came to the top of the waters, then as suddenly as she appeared gasping for air she went back under the waves again. We kept looking and waiting painstakingly for them to rise to the surface again. Suddenly Lil Eric came up with Renee in his arms. Later, Father Joseph came up from under the waves dog paddling to the surface as well.

That water was ferocious and fierce. I know, that I know that God has angels in the gap, looking out for praying mothers. In the Bahamas, we found blood thick love on every end. My mom had a handful of close friends and family members, including our favorite uncle Nung, who was her backbone. Our house was never absent of cousins, friends, visitors or love and laughter. The Bahamas to me was home.

However, my dad moved to Florida along with my two older sisters when I was eight years old. Where he should have paved the way for the rest of the family to come and join him.

However, when we thought he was making a new life for us, he was instead building a new life for himself with another family. Still a year later like planned he sent for my mom, who was now eight months pregnant to come and join him. And in a country where she had no friends, no family, where she knew no one, he up and left for work one day and never came back home. He was the only breadwinner in our household, and he left.

Left the rent two months past due, the water, the lights and the gas bill with final notices and the fridge and the cabinets empty. It would have been so much easier for my mom to just pack up and move back home, to the Bahamas. Except an easy now, was not an alternative to our future best. As far as she was concerned, there was not a choice between the roads of easy and hard. No, there was only one road that led straight ahead. So rather than take the easy way, my mom got up and asked the next-door neighbors about the bus route. Then she went out and found a right now job, a job where she worked as a maid, which was way beneath her. Back in the Bahamas she was a proud preschool teacher

However, this right now job was our ladder. She had a purpose, and she was not turning or looking back. She met with the landlords and made plans to make good on the rent. Next, she caught the bus to each of the utility companies and made arrangements to pay our utilities.

Later, she walked across the streets to Mr. Harry's Grocery Store, a man she had never met before and somehow made arrangement for a store credit. A haughty, proud woman swallowed her pride so that we would not have to go to bed hungry.

Some days, when my mom left for work in the mornings there would be no food in our fridge or cabinets. Cold water with sugar and mayonnaise sandwiches was a blessing for they were something. Dutifully, if my mom made even five dollars in tips, she would often take two buses back home from work during her half an hour lunch break to bring us lunch. My mom was an attractive, thirty-something-year-old woman, living in one of the cheapest one-bedroom apartments in over town with five small children. Just about every weekend our bedroom glass would be smashed by some good for nothing man, attempting to break in.

We had to sleep with a knife under our pillow and a baseball bat beside our bed. But still, my mom had a purpose. She kept her eyes on the prize and stayed in America. About a year later when my Uncle sent my cousin Ken to stay with us the attempts to break into our house abruptly stopped.

The presence of a fourteen-year-old, teenage boy proved safer than no presence of a man at all. Eventually, my mom went back to school at night and became a Nursing Assistant. Later, she furthered her education to become a Medical Assistant

. Many days I saw my mom drained and worn out, having just enough oomph to stagger into bed. One day I asked her, Mommy, why don't we just pack up and move back home? She said "No Nett, you guys can have so much more opportunities over here. A better education, better jobs a more affordable cost of living, a better chance than I had. America is a land of opportunities. Back in the Bahamas, it's not what you know, but who you know. My mom said, "I can't take you all back to that."

"Nett remember, the storm doesn't always rage. I know that one day our sun is going to shine. One day, we're going to be in a better place." She said "I remember standing at our back-door years ago in the Bahamas, looking up at the sky and praying to God. I asked him to open up this door for me to get to America so that I can provide a better future for me, for us.

Baby although it's been hard, I know, that this is our open door." My mother stayed in the race because she had us on her mind and in her heart. She showed us that faith is being faithful unto the death. Faith is never backing down or giving in no matter what Satan throws at us. She showed us that faith has a purpose. She maintained focus.

Even today when me and my sisters are going through really hard times, we remind each other of mommy, who came to a strange country with five small children, no money and no support system. And although faced with devastating adversities she faithfully stood her ground, and stayed focused on her purpose, which was to provide a better life for us. When am driving down the streets, sometimes am reminded of my mom who never owned a car. When I look out my bedroom window, at the soothing lake and tranquil landscape just steps away from my back porch, am reminded of the drug-ravaged neighborhood where we lived and the faithful sacrifice she made for us.

No matter how hard it got, we never heard her talking about looking or turning back. She didn't give herself, or us a plan-B. Plan-A for us as it. God had honored her prayer request in getting us here and we were here sink or swim. Due to her tenacity, we all; apart from my youngest sister have college degrees. This would have been virtually impossible for a single mother to do in the Bahamas.

My younger sister chose her own path. Like that old adage states You can take a horse to the water, but you cannot make him drink. He has to want it. She didn't want it. When we think of mommy, no matter what we're going through we know that against the odds, she did it, and that encourages us to hold fast. Our lives have been made so much smoother because of her diligence. One of her favorite saying was "Where there is a will; there is a way."

At nineteen years old after going to the Bahamas to visit one summer, I finally understood the full concept of my mom's conversation with me at nine years old and was able to truly appreciate the purpose of her sacrifice.

While in the Bahamas, after a long search I found a job paying $150 a week. I was told that I would have to work six days a week from 7 a.m in the morning until the 7 p.m nightly for this measly paycheck.

In addition, a gallon of milk at that time cost about two dollars and change in Florida but nearly doubled that amount in the Bahamas. Everything was doubled the price that I would get it for in Florida, with the exception of Sea Food. For the life of me, I couldn't understand how people could afford this cost of living. When I got back home to Florida, I thanked my mom repeatedly for staying and making a difference for us.

First Corinthians 4-8 states, "Love suffers long and is kind, love does not envy, love does not parade itself, is not puffed up. (5) does not behave rudely, does not seek its own, is not provoked, thinks no evil; (6) does not rejoice in iniquity, but rejoices in the truth; (7) bears all things, believes all things, hopes all things, endures all things. (8) Love never fails." True love has a purpose, agape love is faithful. I realized this to the fullest after I started having kids of my own because my life was no longer just about me but rather about them.

My children became my heart, my dream, and my purpose. My goal in life is to make sure their needs are met. Before I had no charge to keep. My life was all about me. If I were on a job in which I felt shoved, pushed, or disrespected, I wouldn't think twice about leaving. But after having my kids, I could no longer just up and leave because they needed to be provided for. I couldn't imagine me ever not knowing whether they were clean and dry or warm at night. My not knowing that they had a meal before going to bed or that they were sleeping in a safe, warm and comfortable place.

My children changed my focus. They changed my purpose. They changed my way of being because they are my heartbeat. Isaiah 49:15 states, "Can a woman forget her own baby and not love the child she bore? Even if a mother should forget her child, I will never forget you." Isaiah 49:15 (GNT). Psalm 27:10 states, "My father and mother may abandon me, but the Lord will take care of me." Psalm 27:10 (GNT) We may sometimes feel like God has turned his back on us, but just like a good mother, God is always here. He said, "I will never leave you nor forsake you." He said, "I love you with an everlasting love. "Nothing that we do can separate us from his love.

God is faithful and trustworthy. Have you noticed God call Abraham faithful knowing (because he is all knowing) that Abraham would doubt him and birth an Ishmael? Knowing he would laugh within himself and say, "Shall Sarah still bear a child at ninety?"

Although we doubt in our minds, Gods focus is our hearts. (First Samuel 16:7) states, "But the Lord said unto Samuel, look not on his countenance, or on the height of his stature, because I have refused him for the lord seethe not as man seethe; for man looketh on the outward appearance, but the Lord looketh on the heart." Our heart is more concrete than our mind. Our tumultuous minds are constantly trying to reason a thing out that is its nature. The heart is the spirit of a man. It sees a little deeper under the surface.

God saw Abrahams heart. He saw Abrahams craving for an Isaac of his own flesh. He also saw that if he honored that request and then required Abraham to trust him and give Isaac back, Abraham although heartbroken and shattered, would humbly lie Isaac down as a burnt offering. Abraham, giving his best, just as God has given his best, Jesus Christ his only begotten son.

God honors faithfulness that is why he said, but without faith, it is impossible to please him; for he that cometh to God must believe that he is, (exist) and that he is a rewarder of them that diligently seek him. (Heb 11:6) You have to get to know him in order to have faith in him, to know that he is not a man that he should lie, nor the son of man that he should repent. (Num 23:19) states, "Hath he said and shall he not do it? "Or hath he spoken, and shall he not make it good?" We must know in faith that he is the word and that the word is alive. The word is our life, as a child of God. Read (Gen 1) In the beginning, everything he spoke, came into existence.

Moreover, he is the truth, how can he not recognize truth. You have to know that if you trust him, he will save you and that he is sovereign if he says you're blessed, who can say curse. Remember (Num 23:20) Balaam said, "Behold, I have received command to bless; and he hath blessed; and I cannot reverse it." (Num 23:8) He said, "How shall I curse, whom the lord had not cursed?" No matter what Balak offered Balaam he could not curse what God had blessed. "

We have to remember that God is sovereign, judge of all, and creator. God is infinite. As Christians we have to trust that if we so desire to learn of him, he will reveal himself to us, just as he said he would in his word. Scriptures says, draw near to God and he will draw near to you) you make the first move and watch God act. He is gentle, he will not force himself or his faith on you.

However, as you grow in faith, you will learn that if you follow and delight in him, he will give you the desires of your heart. For it is Gods good pleasure to bless you. God is not seeking for our vows or offerings. He is seeking a broken spirit and a contrite heart. Intimacy with us is the desire of his heart. He wants true fellowship. What can we offer him other than ourselves? Other than our whole heart?

He offered up himself for our fellowship. His only begotten son. Him, manifested in the flesh. If he gave all of him, why should he accept any less of us? Therefore, faith is paramount, only in faith can we truly trust him with our whole heart, with our lives. Again, that is why scripture states without faith it is impossible to please God.

Remember God owns everything. We only have what he opens his hands up and allows us to obtain. Everything that we own is already his gifts to us. He does not need his things back; they are freely his to take, if he so pleases or desires. Our very breath, our life is his, but in gentleness, he only takes what is freely given up to him. Mind you if he has called you, you will be tried, tested, and changed. Like Jesus, you will have a wilderness experience. He might start with mediocrity, but he does not dwell in mediocrity.

If he has called you and you continually refuse him, you will be chastened. Like Jonah, you may run for a season but from him, you cannot hide. Because our life belongs to him. He is our creator. Read the Old Testament. God is faithful, but God does not play, with God, you will see that love is sometimes tough.

God wants us at a place where we trust and look up to him and him alone, wholly, and completely whatever our need may be. God wants us to trust him and to have faith in him because he honors faith.

The Bible says to have faith in God, not in self, not in man, nor in the elements or our surroundings. Faith in God moves God. Sometimes our best efforts might fail, but God never fails.

Through faith, God teaches of his faithfulness. If you know and have faith in God, you know that secret place where even death of loved ones or Satan's' evil attacks of deadly illness in our lives, cannot break us. That place where you are enveloped in his perfect peace, his sovereignty, his covering, his blood; because you know that this temporal is destined for the eternal and the sting of death is not your victor.

For truly where the spirit of the lord is, there is liberty. Moreover, in all things, through all things, forever, he is our way of escape, if we have faith in him and maintain focus always on him and not on us, or our circumstances. For if in faith, you accepted and belong to him, then his spirit dwells in, lives in you.

Moreover, you ought to know in whom you believe. As a Christian, you ought to be in that place where you are no longer trusting in you having God, but you ought to know, that you know, that God has you. For he keepeth all his bones, no one can take anyone or anything that has been entrusted unto him. You must get to that place, that presence in Christ and dwell there; under the shadow of his wings, not under your limited understanding. Fellowship promotes growth in faith. Read the stories of David, Daniel, and Moses.

It took faith for Moses to keep going back to a hardened, faithless Pharaoh, while continually receiving untoward results. Yeah, Moses was fearful at first, but he had a lot of faith, he didn't stop going back. After the fogs, and lice, boils, hail, locusts, darkness, the death of their live stocks and ultimately the death of all the firstborn of the Egyptians, he kept going back. In the face of insurmountable adversities, Moses kept turning around and going back.

God knew his intentions were not to just bring them out but to bring them out with great substance, with abundance. However, God does not reveal his entire plan to man. Yet if he says go, we must have faith and obedience enough to say, God if you say go consider me gone. After committing adultery with Bethsheba and murder, in faithfulness, David was wise enough to repent and seek God.

While in pride instead of pursuing God, Saul sought the accolades and praise of men and pursued David. Saul ended up dying by his own sword and David reign as king in his stead. (This did not happen in that order, but it is an example of the different results of faith and praise to God verses faith and praises of men.)

Joshua believed that God had given him Jericho. In faith and obedience, he marched around the city once every day for six days and then seven times on the seventh day, without weapons, instead with instruments of praise and worship. Really, in all honesty, if God commanded, would you have considered God foolish in your wisdom, or would you have taken up your instruments and marched in obedience.

In faith, Gideon went to war with only three hundred men, trusting that Gods army was more than enough. In fact, his three hundred was still too much, because God does not need our earthly armies to do battle. In doing this he is teaching us of his faithfulness, but he is still God of all, all by himself.

Moreover, he does not need our armies, armor, swords, and shields to win no war in heaven or on earth. Look back at Joseph, how many of us would have held fast to our faith after being sold into slavery by our very own family members, those who are supposed to love us. Yet, still while being obedient to God Joseph was falsely accused and thrown into prison. Would you have kept the dream alive?

As Christians, some of us have an attitude not of sonship but of owingness. We think God owes us something, therefore when things do not go our way, our faithlessness immediately shows up. Think ye not that the God who knows our minds, who searcheth the heart of men, know not our motives?

Show up in faith and you will be testifying of Gods faithfulness. Gods faithfulness is not what we in our give me-ness receive but it is trusting in him regardless. It is confidence in whom this life, this existence belongs too, to the death, no matter what. Because if you really gave it to him, this life, your life, why are you constantly taking it back?

Why are you head aching about every little thing that happens? Why aren't you trusting in his being in control, knowing that he knows how to take care of his business?

Our problems, cares, circumstances, our every concern, is now not our business but Gods business. If you are truly trusting in his faithfulness, then stop meddling in his affairs. Just because your limited understanding cannot make sense of it all, does not mean he is lost or confused about it. No, he is just resting, because he has it under control. He has an appointed time for everything and he wants you to rest. That is why in the Psalms he keeps reminding us to Selah, to be still and rest in the lord.

Furthermore, if your desired result does not come through, So, what it is not about you or me. We made it about us, while it should never have stopped being about him. If he died for you, what are you willing to die too for him? Must it always be about us? Must we trust and praise when all is well, in the good times and in the face of adversity and death, curse him and turn away?

Job remembered who God is and was, not just who God was. What if God just loved us when we did well? Who wants love with such limits, what kind of love is that? Is that even love? Are our times supposed to always be favorable? Who of us can live up to those standards, God can, but what man can? True love stands firm and endures in all, through all.
True love is faithful. Are you faithful, while seeking Gods faithfulness?

In hardship, God is trying to show us something about us. He knows us to the core, the marrow, even better than we know ourselves. Are you sure you have been purified or does circumstances and things still have you? Only God knows. He sees the chains that still have to break for you to be whole, steadfast, and free, counting on him now and forever, throughout eternity.

Do you love God enough to allow those chains to be broken? Will you still stand after being a little bend or twisted? Will you allow you to be perfected in him and through him? Remember he is faithful, but while our limited sight is on the temporal, Gods' is on the eternal.

To have faith in him we must know who he is, for if we do not know him, how can we believe in him, and how can we be expecting of him? Faithfulness is a reward of having faith in him.

Joshua and the Israelite children won a battle they did not lift a finger to fight, because they had enough faith in God's faithfulness to walk around Jericho seven times, not with weapons but with instruments of songs and praise.

Gideon won a battle with three hundred men because he trust in Gods faithfulness to go in with the odds stacked against him. He had enough faith to know that if that war was going to be won, God had to be on the front line, and in obedience, he picked up his armor, sword, and shield and fell in line, following his Shepherd to victory.

Moses spent forty years in the desert hiding from the Egyptians, think ye not that he did not know, he was headed towards the Red Sea, a dead end. Nonetheless, he had enough faith to keep going and to stretch forth his staff making a clear path, a way where there seemed to be no way, when instructed to do so.

Again, to see Gods faithfulness we must have faith. We have to know that he is the son of the living (living) God. In addition, we must trust in the fact that he can do anything but fail, scriptures state that there is no failure in God.

We have to know that we can do all things through him who strengthens us. We have to know his word and take him at his word. We must maintain our eyes stayed on him regardless of how ridiculous our circumstance is. Do not try to be wise with God, because God is supernatural.

His ways are not our ways and his thoughts are not our thoughts. So, do not try to trace him, or map him, or figure him out. He is infinite. Instead, our job is simply to learn of him, meditate on the word, relax, rest, trust and have faith in God. Moreover, act when he says to act, instead of always reacting.

Remember God uses the foolish things of the world to confound the wise. (First Corinthians 1:27) With all our knowledge, degrees, accolades, smarts, bank accounts and clouts, you better know, you still ain't got nothing on Jesus, not even a grain of a mustard seed of sense on or over him.

Faith is doing whatever God tells you to do. If God says go, you go. Stay, you stay. Bend you bend. Break, you break. Wake up and pray, you better wake up and pray. Knowing God is in control.

Moreover, God does not make mistakes, whether he calls you for an all-nighter or just a minute out of the day. You pray and pray until he says all is well or stop its okay.

Get to that place in faith where the Shepherd the Holy Ghost dwells in you, and regardless of circumstances, you trust his sovereignty and faithfulness in all he calls and pursues you to do, or go through.

Faith in God is sometimes holding on tight and praying for strength in the senselessness. Although God is faithful, his plans do not come with blueprints or maps, most of the time it is more like a jigsaw puzzle. God is not confused but we are conformed to an earthly way of thinking, to reasoning, to logic. Therefore, we have to be in that place where we are led, held up by grace and not by our own limited understanding.

Remember, anything worth having, we will have to do battle to attain and sustain. You have to make up in your mind what is worth fighting for, things, the temporal or Jesus.

Jesus is worth fighting for. He fought for you straight to the cross, where he laid it all down. So, get your mind off the temporal and have faith in Gods eternal faithfulness. If you live right, trust and have faith, knowing that no matter what, heaven belongs to you, that is what counts.

Do not vacillate. Remember nothing in this world is worth more than Jesus. When it is all over and done, as scripture states, "What does it profit a man to gain the world and lose his soul?" Faith in God is recognizing the true gift, which is Jesus Christ birth, life, death and resurrection for you and me.

The true gift is eternal life with God. We cannot afford to let this temporal take our minds off the eternal. We must have faith in God. I prayed, and my mother died. I prayed, my daughter died. Does that mean God is not faithful? Did God promise us forever in this life here on earth? No, a man born of a woman will die and after this, the judgment, after this, eternal life. They did not come here to stay (my mother and daughter) the mere fact that God counted me worthy of the gifting of their presence, was faithful of him. The joy of sharing in their existence, was an act of benevolence on his behalf, in my life.

Remember he gives us to our biological families. Yes, a man born of a woman is not promised any bed of roses in this life. Job says man born of a woman will have trouble in this world. As sheep of his pasture, the Bible warns in (Romans 8:36) "For thy sake we are killed all the day long; we are accounted as sheep for the slaughter".

In (John 15:20) Jesus said, "Remember the word that I said unto you, the servant is not greater than his Lord. If they have persecuted me, they will also persecute you; if they have kept my saying, they will keep yours also."

I will re-emphasize that we are in a fight and as a soldier, we must put on the whole armor of God, and keep it on until the battle is over. (The Holy Ghost) We cannot afford to fall asleep and lie down our sword. In war there is no fair fight, everyone is fighting to win, and steadfastly looking for an opportunity to sneak in and conquer the enemy.

As Christians, we are not promised pure golden lives or grasses of pure green. No, we were reminded, that it rains on the just as well as the unjust. However, God is with us. The great promise, our exceeding great reward has always been Jesus Christ sacrifice for our eternal life. We have somehow, like Adam and Eve, as humans lost focus. It's sad most of us do not even recognize this.

How did it, salvation, become more about us than about him? Was not we suppose to lie down our lives and pick up his cross and follow him? Instead, we are trying to have him follow us. Remember though he was beaten, spit on, mocked, persecuted, and weighted down with that cross, in faithfulness, Jesus kept getting back up, baring the weight of this world, to Calvary, to the grave, and to hell, until he rose on the third day. He maintained focus. He was born to live and die for our salvation and our impartation of the Holy Spirit and he was faithful unto the death.

He came to give, why are we all about receiving? The real question is not about Jesus, Gods faithfulness but rather our faith, our focus, our faithlessness. We are so ready to reign with him in heaven and on earth but who is really willing to suffer with him? Christianity is not, just a crutch, it is sometimes a cross. Yet we must not put it down. Jesus said, "pick up your cross and follow me." (Luke 9:23) Remember, Jesus was crucified for doing absolutely nothing wrong. Are we willing to stand up for him only in the good times or in all times, no matter what? Is our whole heart in this or just the part that is being gratified; just that part that is receiving?

Have we placed a long pause after certain earthly means or a question mark if we do not attain certain dreams? Is our relationship with him free, pure, and whole or does it come with limited warranties, that our minds and hearts control? Do we have faith or just our agendas?

Remember without faith it is impossible to please God and thereby receive from God. Faithfulness is a reward of having and maintaining faith in God, no matter what. Note, Job did not give up after the loss of his processions and kids, although his wife encouraged him too, he maintained focus. He remembered who God is and God in turn sat and talked with him, and then gave him back more than he ever had before. For God is faithful.

It's Still All or Nothing

ABOUT THE AUTHOR

Jannette Holt is a Registered Nurse by profession. Her passion and desires are to not only see, but to experience the fullness, the more that Jesus said the Church would experience when he ascended to heaven. Her desire is to entice the Church to become thirsty and hungry for God, so that we his body can set this world ablaze for his Glory